MONEY MAGIC

EASY AND SURPRISING WAYS TO NOT BE BROKE

DUNCAN MACLEOD

Books That Save Lives

Published by BTSL/Jim Dandy Publishing
6252 Peach Avenue
Van Nuys, CA 91411
info@jimdandypublishing.com

For bulk orders, special quantities, course adoptions, and corporate sales, please email info@jimdandypublishing.com

ISBN: (print) 978-1-963667-28-8 (ebook) 978-1-963667-25-7

Printed in the United States

BISAC: BUS050030, EDU013000, BUS050010, BUS027030

Printed in the United States of America

CONTENTS

FOREWORD

BECCA ANDERSON, BESTSELLING
AUTHOR OF BADASS AFFIRMATIONS

My first money miracle lesson from Duncan was when we met in the Lower Haight and were both making a rather meager living as new entries into the working world. Shout out to the late, great Louise Hay, who helped inspire the Money Miracle Muse! Duncan gifted me his well-worn cassette tape of her speaking about how to develop a mindset of abundance. I admittedly brought a bit of a scarcity mindset to California with me from West Virginia and was eager to learn new ways. I loved Louise Hay's insights, which were wholly new to me. Duncan patiently explained to me his takeaways from Hay's wisdom and how it had worked for him, changing his life for the better. When paying bills, instead of resenting the utility that had generously supplied water and electricity, you should write the check, seal the envelope, and say aloud "Thank you, Pacific Gas and Electric, for supplying me with power for my home and trusting me to pay you. Blessings to you, PG&E!"

We even began a ritual of paying bills together and then walking to the mailbox, where we would pronounce our gratitude to all the recipients of our money. We even added the finishing touch of kissing the stamped envelopes and saying "Thank you!" before dropping them in for mailing. We got some looks of surprise at our mailbox rituals, but we believed whole-heartedly in Louise Hay, and doing that had been working for Duncan. Soon, it began to work for me, and I fully embraced the mindset. Most surprising of all, I stopped being filled with dread and worry when bills came in and started paying them the same day, when-ever possible. In addition to adopting an attitude of abundance, it helped my credit score!

In the early 1990s, we had to go to the mailbox for our 5-minute gratitude ritual. Nowadays, with all the instantaneous ways of sending money and electronic payments, it might be closer to a 5-second ritual. How-ever, before you hit "send", get into your Manifestor's Mindset and express thanks before you click or tap. This attitude of abundance that stems from the mindset is like a muscle; the more you use it, the stronger it will be, and you will see many manifestations.

All these years later, Duncan is my accountant and has abetted many other money miracles that en-abled me to buy a house in Northern California. And I have had robust book sales of over a million copies, which is truly miraculous!

I give Duncan MacLeod's book my highest recom-mendation. It reads like your kind and wise friend of-fering you helpful tips and a lot of common sense. With Duncan's guidance, you, too, can have an abundant life!

INTRODUCTION BY AUTHOR

MY STORY

My journey and relationship with money began at the age of 11 when I got my paper route. I learned a lot about hard work, but nothing about smart work. I'm a child of divorce, and living with a single, oft-unemployed mother taught me a lot about the perils and pitfalls of money, but nothing about the way money really works. Neither of my parents had a clue how to acquire wealth. We even bought a house and sold it for less than we paid!

When I was young, the stock market was not really accessible like it is now. I would have needed a broker and would have had to pay a hefty commission to buy stock. I actually asked my mother in 1978 how to invest in Apple. A friend with wealthy parents had a visit from a guy they affectionately called "Woz". He left a computer overnight. It was a wooden box with a partially eaten apple emblazoned on the wood. It came with a tape recorder and a box of cassettes full of programs. My friend and I hacked it (we were told not to touch it, but come on!) We played a Star Wars-themed game all night. The next morning, when Steve Wozniak came to collect his prototype computer, he was surprised to learn that two dumb kids had figured out how to entertain themselves with his wooden box. He told me to buy some shares, but I didn't know how, and my paper route only earned me 10 dollars a month. My mother barely had two quarters to rub together. My friend's dad offered to loan me the money for five shares if I asked my mother. She came back with a resounding, "No f**ing way." And so I missed out on the opportunity of a lifetime.

I was curious about the finance pages in the newspaper. Every afternoon, the evening paper listed rows and rows of letters and fractional numbers. It looked quite odd. A stock might be listed as BOA 10 3/16. I asked my mother what the letters and numbers meant. She said, "I have no idea." And that was that for the next 25 years. I remained completely oblivious to the stock market and all that it had to offer because no one around me could say what the letters and fractional numbers meant!

It turns out the letters were the code for the name of a stock, and the numbers were prices! Why didn't they just say "Bank of America closed at $10.19?" Why would prices be listed in fractions of 1/16? The 3-4 letter codes were because otherwise the stocks wouldn't line up neatly in columns. As for the wacky price, it goes back to the Spanish gold currency (doubloons) in the days when coins were literally broken into pieces of eight. And when more money was circulating in the 20th century, they broke it down even further into 1/16. I think the very wealthy wanted things to stay that way, keeping the riff-raff (us) from trying to trade on the market. At least it felt that way once I finally learned how it all worked.

Nowadays, anyone with an internet connection can go online and find out in less than a second how much a given stock is selling for. You can find it out as many times as you can click refresh on your browser. And you can buy, sell, and trade stocks if you have an online brokerage account. The democratization of the stock market is one of the best innovations of the internet age. Even with the chaos we're seeing as of the printing of this book, there is no better way to have wealth. I'll explain this more in the chapters on wealth and investing.

In my late teens, I ended up on a psychiatric ward and spent a few years getting my mental wellness under control. I lived on public assistance, but managed to go back to college and earn a dual bachelor's degree in Film and Italian. I came to Hollywood to make it big (and made it small). I lost quite a few jobs, scraped bottom dozens of times, and basically failed to get my sh*t together. I found a program called Debtors Anonymous. Then it changed.

That's the sad portion of my story. Everyone's is different. I've learned a lot since then. I got my MBA, invested in the markets, bought a house, and started coaching people how to turn their financial life around. It started with a crisis. I lost my job due to the World Trade Center attacks on 9/11. I had a 401(k) and needed to "roll it over". I didn't have a replacement job, so I went to "American Express Financial Services" and got my first advisor. She taught me how it all works. She took my measly 401(k) and rolled it into an IRA. (Don't worry if this seems boring to some of you, it may make more sense later.) Ameriprise, as it's called now, has helped me grow my pittance of an IRA into a surprisingly large pile of money. Each time I quit a job, I'd put the 401(k) into the IRA, and voilà! My advisor is a friend and trusted counselor. I'll talk more about the importance of finding such a friend in Chapter Ten.

This book is for the person who is still struggling to understand the difference between wealth and income. Their eyes glaze over when someone talks about stocks. Or maybe they have credit card or student loan debt and fear they'll never get ahead of it. Maybe they are having trouble earning and saving money, deciding between paying rent, eating, or paying their bills. It's also for the children of wealthy parents who want or need to make their own way in the world. Really, the book is for anyone who feels they're missing some information about money. I'm going to give a lightning-fast overview of how money works, how to increase it, how to be 'wealthy', and how to do it easily, smarter, without breaking your back at a thankless, low-paying job. Throughout the book you will find "Money Miracles" - quick and easy ways to get a hold of your finances and make positive steps toward financial freedom. I originally planned to call this book, "Guncle Duncan's Magic Money Book". But many readers might not know what a Guncle is. It's an uncle, but a little more fabulous and witty than your other uncles. I'm a gay uncle. As an only child, when I realized that I was gay, I had to give up something. I would never get to be "Uncle Duncan." I wasn't able to marry another man, so legally I couldn't be an uncle. When gay marriage came along, I married a wonderful man. We've been together for 23 years as of the writing of this book, and we've been married for 12 years. A few years back, I suddenly realized that I was a Guncle. My husband has nieces, nephews, and even grand-nieces and grand-nephews. I'm Uncle Duncan! It inspired me to write this book for them. I hope it helps all of you nieces and nephews who need a fun gay uncle who also happens to know a few things about how money works!

So read on. As you can see, this is a very short book. I don't go into detail or depth with most of the concepts. Instead, I repeat the important concepts in different chapters. It's sort of a cheat sheet to get you financially literate. It's the kind of book you can read on your phone while you wait for your lunch, your bus, or your coffee. But I'll talk more about that coffee in Chapter Two. First, let's talk about the word 'wealth' and what it really means.

CHAPTER 1
WHAT IS WEALTH?

WEALTH

This is simple. First, what ISN'T wealth. Wealth isn't income from your job. Wealth isn't a yacht, a Lamborghini, or a Patek-Philippe watch. Yes, there's value in income and possessions, but they aren't wealth, and I'll explain why.

Wealth is the state in which you earn money without doing anything. That's right, you do NOTHING and you get an income. It can be as simple as a savings account with interest, or as complex as rents, royalties, dividends, or annuities. The important takeaway is that when your money and property begets more money with little or no effort, that is wealth income. You may also hear it called passive income. But I call it wealth.

Earned income is money you have to work hard to make. You sell your time and services to an employer or clients, and you bring in money. But you can't kick back and enjoy the money, you have to keep working. Unless you invest the money, you're never going to be in a state of wealth.

You can have a million-dollar annual income, but if you fail to invest it, and you spend more than you make, you're actually in a state of poverty.

• • •

BUY NICE THINGS THAT LAST

Some things increase in value, while others decline. The latter is far more common. A new car drops in value immediately after you drive it off the lot, but its value to you is lasting. So buy the cheapest but safest car you can stand, so your purchase lasts longer. Clothing holds value for you as the person wearing it, but you can't sell it at a profit. Do you really need to buy new clothes every season? Furniture, cookware, appliances, and other things will lose all their value over time. Yes, you want a comfortable home, a good place to prepare meals, and clean clothes. So get good quality things that will last a long time. Don't buy a new couch because you're tired of the old one; buy it because your current one has finally become uncomfortable. If you're struggling to repay debts, you might have a friend who is always buying new couches; counsel them not to and ask if you can have the old one!

Examples of things that could increase in value might be a very rare sports car, a vacation house, gold, fine jewelry, stamps, or possibly even a really high-quality watch. When they do, that thing has generated wealth. But most of them are risky investments at best. Think about how much you spend on servicing a rare sports car to keep it in sellable shape. Is it going to be less than you make, should you ever sell it? Jewelry goes out of style, housing markets fall, insurance and taxes go up, and yes, the stock market can crash. Great, you say. So there's no point in trying, right?

Wrong!

PENNIES MAKE PENNIES

The stock market tends to fool people into believing that the way you make money is "buy low and sell high". Yes, that will make you money, but it's a gamble, so you can lose a lot, too. When you invest in stocks, the real income comes as dividends, which is the money the company pays you because you own a little piece of their profits. You own a piece of a business, and you don't have to do a thing. The CEO and all of the employees do the hard work of running the business, while you collect a piece of the profits. A lot of people think the wealth is the stock itself, and they're partly right. But read on to see where this is partly mistaken.

The mistake we make is buying a stock because it might increase in value. If you look at the money you paid for the stock, and then its price goes down during a downswing, you're going to feel like you lost money. But if you look at the money the stocks pay out, then you're looking at real wealth. And what goes down usually goes up over time, so you haven't really lost that money, as long as you hold on to the stock and don't sell it. The only risk here, and it's very slight, is if a company declares bankruptcy. This happens once in a great while. You lose all of the value of the stock (and any upcoming dividends). That happens, so it's important not to put all your financial eggs in one basket. That's why there are mutual funds, which are a diversified basket of stocks. Even taking market crashes into consideration, these funds consistently increase in value by at least 7% per year over the course of ten years. And they pay dividends!

There are other forms of wealth, too. If you're a musician, writer, or artist, the money you make from your works can be wealth. Putting on a concert is a great deal of work, and a source of earned income, but your songs and recordings earn royalties. They are wealth because you don't do anything to earn that portion of your income, it's passive. Writing a book takes a few months or years, and the advance is earned income. But the income from the books may require very little work once it's flowing. That's wealth. Whether it's ten bucks a year or a million a month, royalties are wealth income, not earned income.

Similarly, if you own an apartment building, and the

rent you take in is more than the mortgage, insurance, and upkeep, then it's wealth. But if you are on site managing the property every day, it starts to look a lot more like earned income. When you make enough to let a property management company do most of the work, you're looking at wealth.

The growth and big-name tech stocks grow, but many are reinvesting their earnings and not paying you any dividends. Stocks in old-school companies that pay dividends regularly are basically rock-solid sources of wealth income. I'm not allowed to go into details about which stocks are good and which are bad. Only a certified advisor can offer that sort of advice. That's something you'll ask when you find your aforementioned financial advisor, which I will mention throughout the book. I give you the complete lowdown on advisors in the last chapter, Chapter 10.

Some of you might say "huh? I'm 20 years old and I'm a part time student with barely any income. How would I find a financial advisor?" You can begin your relationship with an advisor at any time. They may give you some goals to achieve before you start working with them. But you can start the relationship any time.

Is Your Debt Secured Or Unsecured?

Debt comes in two flavors: secured or unsecured. Secured debt is backed up by a guarantee. Huh? You buy a car with a loan that guarantees the car dealer can take back the car if you don't pay. When that happens, you don't owe anything any more. Same with a home loan.

I make this distinction so you understand this: another key component of wealth is that your unsecured debt is minimal, and does not ever exceed your cash. By unsecured debt I mean credit cards, student loans, personal loans, or any other form of debt that isn't guaranteed or secured. That debt lingers when you stop paying because it is not secured. You can't give back your education or that watch you bought with your credit card. (Okay, you can return a watch, but that's a bad habit).

Secured debt, as I mentioned, is a car or house loan. The debt vanishes the moment you surrender the car or house.

By cash, I mean paper money, checking, savings, stocks, bonds, or any other means to pay for something almost immediately. This is sometimes called "liquid savings".

Stocks and bonds are not quite as "liquid" as checking, savings or cash, but they can be sold the same day you need cash. I am not talking about retirement accounts, life insurance, houses, cars, or other holdings that delay your ability to pay; they are not cash.

Why is this important? Because most unsecured debt has an interest rate that far exceeds what you can make by investing or saving. You're paying out more than you're taking in. Your wealth is being devoured by your unsecured debt. Here's a simple diagram that shows why unsecured credit destroys wealth.

Concept:

If your credit card charges you 29.9% interest over the course of a year, and your investments are growing and paying 7.9%, that means you're effectively losing 22% a year in interest! Huh?

STOCKS AND BONDS

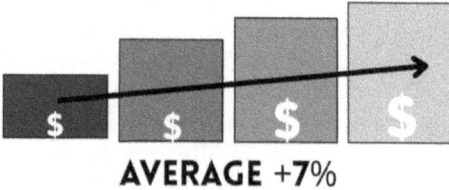

AVERAGE +7%

VS

CREDIT CARD

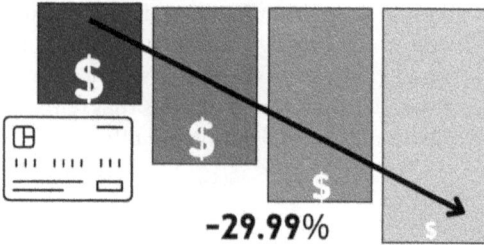

−29.99%

Why is secured debt different? With debt secured by property, such as a house or car, you have an unappealing option, but an important one. If you can't make payments on your house, and you stop, the payments go away completely when the bank forecloses. You don't owe anything more. You've lost a house, but you're free of the house payments. Some people call this "good debt". The interest rates on car and home loans vary over time, but they are often much lower than credit cards or even student loans.

Here's the reason why unsecured debt is so nasty:

STUDENT LOANS

When a student loan goes into default, it NEVER GOES AWAY. You will owe that money for the rest of your life. Your parents might even get nailed. The bank can't repossess your education.

CREDIT CARDS

Credit cards can be negotiated, but you will likely end up paying most or all of the debt at some point. I talk about ways around it in chapter 3. The USA no longer has debtor's prisons, but there are courts that will hold you to payments. So you must have the means to pay your unsecured debt in full before you can say you're actually wealthy.

TAKEAWAYS:

- Wealth income occurs when your money and property work for you, generating more money with little to no effort.
- Earned income is money you have to work for. It is a means to acquire wealth. It is NOT wealth.
- Some possessions, like fine art or antiques, are potential investments, but they only accumulate value; they don't pay you money.

- Unsecured debt erodes your wealth and rarely goes away.
- Secured Debt is only better because it can go away the moment you return whatever you used to secure debt.

CHAPTER 2
FIRST THINGS FIRST - TRIAGE

KNOW YOUR SITUATION

At least half of you are carrying credit card balances that carry over month by month, increasing, and incurring interest charges.

- 52% of the people reading this are earning less than what they're spending each month.
- Over 40% have no liquid savings (money in the bank that you can spend).
- At least 60% of you have no retirement savings.
- 5 million Americans have no bank account at all.

What's important is that all of these are bad things that can be turned around.

First, we need to perform some triage. This means reviewing your earnings and expenses to determine how much is coming in and how much is going out. I created this book so you can read it on a phone; therefore, I won't go through a worksheet. I'm going to tell you to look up a few money management apps and figure out which one will do the trick. The three I am aware of at the moment are NerdWallet, Quicken Simplifi, and YNAB (You Need a Budget). These apps link to your banks and cash apps, suck up all your account balances, expenses, and income and give you nearly an instant snapshot of where you're at. You're either overspending or you're not. If you're getting dinged with interest charges, they'll tell you immediately how much that is.

This book and these apps will work best for individuals with a steady paycheck, credit cards, and bank accounts. If you earn cash, have no credit, or don't have a bank account, I am going to write a different book specifically for you. However, most of this book still covers all the concepts you need to know to plan your path to financial freedom, and you should read on. Perhaps consider waiting to get an app.

Once you've set up the app and all your accounts, watched all the helpful YouTube videos you can find, and have generally gotten a hold of your finances, the rest of this chapter will make more sense. You may want to pause your reading here and look into a finance app now. Gather your logins and passwords, connect your accounts, fix the randomly categorized ice cream cone purchase that shows as a taxi ride, and come back to finish this chapter. You can skip ahead, but as your Guncle, I strongly recommend you take the hour to get this clear picture of your finances.

MONEY MIRACLE

TAKING CONTROL

If you have online access to your financial institutions, this single step will blow your mind. Get a finance-tracking app. You can try NerdWallet, Quicken Simplifi, or YNAB (You Need A Budget), but just be aware that they might disappear, like Intuit's Mint app did. It was replaced with Credit Karma, which is okay, but not as powerful as the two I mentioned. Here's the miracle:

1. Read up on money management apps using AI and search engines.
2. Download the app that you think might work best for you.
3. Gather all your online account logins having to do with money, like your banks, credit cards, and cash apps like PayPal and Venmo.
4. Follow the steps to connect them, one by one.
5. If you hit a snag, go back to the search engine and troubleshoot the issue.
6. The app will categorize all your expenses, either by asking questions or just guessing on its own; verify and recategorize as needed

You just took control of your finances. Have a celebratory cup of your favorite beverage!

. . .

KNOWLEDGE IS POWER

You've taken my advice and didn't skip ahead to further chapters. Good for you! You're about to learn a few quick, dirty tricks that will turn your finances around. The trick takes a minute or two, but it may take a year or two to fully recover, depending on the circumstances. If you're underearning and not getting paid enough, Chapter 6 has more secrets to help you address that. If you're a high earner with a little debt, this could be as short as a two-month recovery process. For the 60% who are carrying balances and bleeding money every month, just trust that what I'm telling you will solve your money worries if you persevere.

Look at the categories in your money management app called late fees, bank charges, and finance charges. These categories show instantly that your earnings are vanishing like a puff of smoke in a cloud of missing money. How much is it? Is it $30.00 per month? $100.00? $1,000.00? Hey! That should be your money, and yet the banks are making you pay through the nose because they handed you some debt, or you were late on a few payments. They didn't even charge you up front to borrow money; they gracefully let you go into debt for free. And now you're giving those a-holes a bunch of money that should have belonged to you.

I have some controversial solutions in Chapter 3, but here we're going to just get you into triage.

DISCRETIONARY VERSUS FIXED (NON-DISCRETIONARY)

I'm going to be using these terms quite a bit in this chapter, so let me define them in simple terms:

Discretionary expenses are those expenses that you can reduce or eliminate without dying. You can still be comfortable when you get rid of them. You won't freeze or starve to death if you stop. One young client asked if

Spotify was discretionary. After holding my tongue and counting to ten, I patiently said, "Yes, that's discretionary."

Fixed or Non-discretionary expenses are mandatory costs to remain alive and able to get to and from your place of work. This will include some expenses that can be reduced, but cannot be eliminated. Groceries. Shelter. Internet. Health Insurance. Utilities. Health Care. Basic clothing. These are non-discretionary. Be sure to remember the difference as we move through this chapter. Here's what you're going to do next:

Freeze Your Credit, Literally!

When you get home, or if you're home already, do this now. Take all of your credit cards out of your wallet, put them in a freezer-safe container full of water, and stick it in your freezer. Do it now, and don't ask questions. Do NOT freeze your debit card(s). You'll need those for the next step.

RECURRING EXPENSES

Next, look at your finance tracking app. If you foolishly skipped that step, you will now need to log onto your banks and credit card providers' websites and manually identify all the different types of expenses you're making. Or, you can simply look at the pie chart on your app because you listened and did what I asked above.

Some of you might be freaking the f*** out right about now. It's okay to take a breather here. If you're cool, keep going. If you're feeling panicky, take a break and come back.

When you've established that you won't be freaking out, get out a notepad. This is a multi-step exercise.

Step One - Recurring Charges

Recurring charges are subscriptions, memberships, bills, and other weekly, monthly, quarterly, or yearly charges. Write down each recurring charge. Got them? All of them? Even those Venmo and Apple Pay charges that you might not have been able to connect to your app? Good. Here's what's happening next. It's going to suck. Again, a brief break is fine, but it should last only until the panic subsides.

You're going to look only at those recurring weekly, monthly, bimonthly, quarterly, and annual charges and figure out which ones are luxuries. Are you going to two gyms? Are you subscribing to design software you haven't used since last year? Is it a meal delivery service that sits untouched in your fridge every week until you toss it out and take the next delivery? You know what I'm talking about when you see them. You get a strange feeling in your gut. You think, "Oh, I deserve this," or "Oh, I might use this someday." But there's this twinge of guilt. Like, maybe you really shouldn't be spending that money. When it's an electric bill, you're not going to feel that twinge of guilt. If you're getting fresh vegetables delivered to your door and using them every week to eat healthily, you should feel proud, not guilty. You're going to identify the guilt-inducing charges for the next step by putting a tick mark next to them.

This is the sucky part. You're going to cancel those recurring charges. You're going to pick a gym and get rid of it (or both if you're working out at home). You're going to cancel that subscription to Canva you used once to make birthday invitations for a friend three years ago and haven't used since. You're going to decide which of the music platforms you listen to most and chuck the other ones. You're going to cancel those streaming services that you only watch once a year when your favorite series drops.

Here's what you aren't going to do. You won't get rid of everything. You'll keep a gym membership if you're using it. You'll keep your favorite streaming platform that you watch every night. This is triage, it isn't intensive care. If you can't balance your spending after this first trim, then you'll have to get more austere. You are at an income level, and you must live within your means if you want to accumulate wealth.

What you're left with are two things: discretionary and non-discretionary recurring charges.

Step Two – The Great Migration

As mentioned above, fixed (non-discretionary) expenses are the things you truly cannot live without. Rent. Electricity. Water. Therapy. Groceries. Food subscriptions that you truly use. Health insurance. You get the picture. These are the recurring charges that keep you warm, safe, healthy, and comfortable.

Debit cards are just a convenient way to pay from your checking account and nothing more. They're the poorly dressed country cousin to the sharp city-slicker credit cards. But they're important right now. They are your best alternative, and they will move you closer to wealth.

Whether or not you need it to live, you will need to migrate those recurring charges off your credit cards onto your debit cards. If you're going to bounce checks (okay, that's an old-fashioned term for overdrawing and going into negative balance), then you can't move everything yet. Move the ones you know you can afford. You will have to revisit this step a few times as we nudge your budget.

By migrating, I mean visiting the website where you signed up and updating the payment method from a credit card to a debit card. Don't be reckless as you do this. If you're spending a thousand dollars more than you earn every month, you can't move it all at once. I want to emphasize this point, so I'll repeat myself. Do it in stages, and return to this step as you've eliminated a few unnecessary expenses or increased your earnings, which I discuss a little later in the book.

Step Three - Non-Recurring Charges

Once you have all your recurring charges, including utilities, you should look at expenses you make yourself, rather than passively letting someone do it for you by charging a card or pulling it out of your checking.

These are things like:

Food
Clothing
Entertainment
Booze
Coffee

Some advisors might tell you that everything else is discretionary, meaning you can choose not to spend it, and you should probably stop. Those advisors are not entirely wrong, but they're pretty close to entirely wrong. There are plenty of irregular expenses that are core to meeting your basic needs. The most obvious one is groceries.

Food

What's discretionary about groceries is where you shop, how often you choose to cook, and what you buy. Depending on where you live and how much you cook, it might be a few hundred dollars a month, or it might be a lot more. The flip side, of course, is restaurants. So, write down how much of your expenses are for groceries and how much are for restaurants. Put a star next to the coffee house and takeaway expenses. Alcohol and bars are not restaurants, so unless you will have the DTs when you skip a day of drinking, don't include them here.

300-Dollar Haircuts

It doesn't matter if you're a senator or a school-teacher; nobody needs a 300-dollar haircut. Inflation may prove me wrong, but a barber or a neighborhood salon can make you look snappy for under 50 bucks. You're going to have to stop getting your lashes done for a while. You'll need to buy your cosmetics at the drug store, not the department store. I'm sorry if this is a slap in the face to everything you believe, but unless you're spending a lot less than you're earning, this is a budgetary must. Don't stop getting your haircuts, just suck it up and go to the place on Yelp with 4.7 stars and a single dollar sign. And go every two months, not once a week. Sorry to be a downer. This budget buster is something I see with a lot of my clients who identify as female. Societal pressures be damned, you need to take charge of your money, and this is one place where you can.

The Coffee House Problem

I don't know how many of you buy your coffee at a coffee house. It's a great place to catch up with friends, have a treat, wake up, and start your day. Yes, it is all those things. But did you know that they sell coffee you can make at home? Sorry, that was meant to come out in a kind way, but it probably reads a little sarcastic and patronizing. Give your Guncle a break. I'm making a point. Let me do it with dollars and cents.

Last time I went to Starbucks, I spent $8.00 for a decaf iced Americano because they no longer sell "decaf regular coffee," and that's what I like to drink. It still has enough caffeine to make me rattle around like a bee in the window. However, the point is that I just said it costs $8.00. Do you know how much that would cost if I made it at home? Probably about 30 cents. No, seriously. Ice is free, and the single-serve coffee I use costs about 30 cents a cup. Okay, the milk might be another 10 cents. So let's round up and say my coffee costs no more than 50 cents. That's $7.50 less. And if I were able to get my coffee at my former workplace, it would be free. I'd save $8.00. But I work from home now. So scratch that, but keep it in your hat for future use.

Now, imagine what would happen if you put that $7.50 in a jar on any day you stay home and don't go to the coffee house. How much would you have at the end of the month? In fact, let's say you only do this 20 out of 30 days. If you went to the coffee house on the other 10 days, you'd have $150.00 sitting in the jar.

Now, imagine next that you buy some stock with that $150.00. You deposit the cash into your ATM, log on to your online brokerage, and invest the cash in 5 shares of a high-quality, undervalued stock that pays dividends. Whoa! You just got some wealth there. But... do you have credit card debt? Slap that $150.00 down on the credit card first. You want to jam as much money down those bankers' throats as you can. It's the only way to break free. If you're out of debt, then invest it by all means. I'll show you why in an upcoming segment.

MONEY MIRACLE

LOVE COFFEE

A client of mine who worked from home had a coffee habit. Every morning, after checking her emails, she would leave her desk and head to a local chain coffee establishment to get her oat milk latte. She was so busy at work, and the time away from her desk felt sacred. No matter that the coffee cost $8.00, and she did it every day and most weekends. When I pointed out that this was costing her at least $200.00 per month or about $2,400.00 per year, she saw the light.

But how was she going to get by without her oat milk latte? What would she do for a break? Enter her husband. He said, "I can make you an oat milk latte before I leave for work." He studied the recipe and landed on the following:

3 tbsp ground coffee
2 cups of boiling water
¼ cup oat milk

He bought a little hand blender to foam up the oat milk. While brewing a cup of old-fashioned joe using a French press, he put the oat milk in a tiny saucepan and heated it, using the blender to generate foam. When the oat milk had foamed, he'd pour it into a cup and slowly add the coffee. In just two minutes, he had a fresh oat milk latte that cost about 45 cents! Can you imagine the difference? Instead of spending $200.00 per month, she was spending less than $15.00! Of course, as a special treat on most weekends, she would still go out and get herself a coffee. And during the week, she spent the newfound extra time before her first meeting walking around the neighborhood. She still does. She calls that homemade oat milk latte "Love Coffee." And it is indeed a wonderful expression of love from her husband.

———————

. . .

Do You Save?

I said to plunk down $150.00 on a credit card or stock, but I left out an important vehicle that everyone should have - a savings account. They give lousy interest in most cases, but they are a great place to stash money away for emergencies. If you don't have one, simply log on to your bank's website, click a few buttons, and you'll have one. It's linked to your checking, so you can just transfer cash with two clicks. You are usually limited as to how many times you can move money out of savings each month, but you aren't usually penalized for sweeping money in as many times as you like. This savings account won't solve any problems right away, but it will set you up for chapters 4 and 8, so do it now. It literally takes five minutes, and you can do it on your phone.

Okay, I gave you quite a few tasks. Doing them will keep you from bleeding out, but we still have to get you into surgery. The triage portion is over.

TAKEAWAYS

- A finance app is going to help you quickly figure out where your money is going.
- You know which discretionary expenses are just BS because you'll feel guilty
- You can't do a whole lot about non-discretionary expenses at this moment, so don't even shed a tear over them
- Fancy coffee is a privilege, not a right.
- Fancy hairdos are way out of reach for 90% of you, so knock it off!
- Opening a savings account is easy and will

help you with lots of other to-dos in the upcoming chapters.

TO DO:

- Freeze your credit cards in the freezer. I'll explain exactly why in the next chapter
- Download an App and let it suck all your banking info into its belly
- Review the expenses and correct any miscategorizations (it will get 85-95% of them right, by the way)
- Analyze your discretionary and non-discretionary recurring purchases
- Cancel a great deal of your recurring, useless, or luxurious, discretionary, recurring expenses
- Migrate as many of the non-discretionary recurring expenses as possible to your debit card. Do not set yourself up to scrape bottom. You can revisit this step later to finish it all up.
- Next, evaluate your discretionary one-offs, such as haircuts, coffee, restaurants, and, yes, even groceries. Reduce them. You cannot get rid of groceries, and you shouldn't do away with restaurants altogether
- Open an online savings account. Leave it be for now. Just open it.
- Make your coffee at home

CHAPTER 3
THE CREDIT CARD
DATING GAME

THE FREEZER

So why did I tell you to stick your credit cards in the freezer, you ask? Here's why:

Because of interest charges, unless you have a zero balance on your cards at the end of the month, you're losing money. The only way you're going to get out of debt is to migrate your accounts from credit cards to debit cards and stop using those cards for incidentals. It's too tempting to carry them around with you, but there are times when you will need them.

You will likely need credit cards if a big, unexpected expense hits you and there's no way to cover it, pay your rent, and afford food. You want to protect yourself from impulse purchases, but if you cannot find any other way to pay a big bill, then you can consider thawing the card and using it. It's not enough to put it in a drawer for safekeeping. It's too easy to open the drawer and use it without a second thought. When you're waiting for a big block of ice to melt, you'll have time to think about other strategies for managing a big bill or unexpected expense. The goal is to return the cards to the freezer before they thaw. If they thaw, you use that card for the one emergency, then freeze it again. Sounds wacky, right? It works. I did it.

This is a sad story, but I share it with my clients. My father developed a worsening case of Alzheimer's disease. He lived 400 miles from me, so I wasn't able to care for him directly. I relied on a caregiver firm that had hired some very shady caregivers. Two of them were predators. One of them, I'll call her Sharon, told my father that she was his wife. She asked him to take her to fancy meals. She took him to the ATM, where he withdrew all his cash for the month. Monitoring his bank account from afar, I couldn't figure out what was going on! So I drove up there and found this woman 'dating' my poor father, who knew no better. Another caregiver, I'll call her Ida, was sleeping on my father's couch because she was between homes. Sharon had coached her to tell him she was his roommate.

Because there was a chance he might need them in an emergency, I put his credit cards in an unmarked container filled with water and stored them in the freezer. But the damage was done. He'd emptied his retirement account and racked up $20,000.00 in credit card debt. His rent checks bounced, and I had to step in and start paying any bills that Social Security wouldn't cover.

Sharon had been fired from the caregiving agency, but she was still making phone calls. I got chills listening to a message in a sexy voice that said, "Hi, I can't wait to see you on Thursday." I called the cops, and they issued a restraining order. They didn't have enough evidence to prosecute Sharon, so she got away with stealing my Dad's future.

I hired a new caregiver who was the picture of integrity. She shooed away anyone who showed up to take advantage of my father, and I was able to sleep easy. She is still a trusted member of my chosen family. She knew where the cards were because I told her, and she never once had to thaw them. I paid off his credit cards, covered his rent, and supported him until he transitioned to a board and care facility.

Freezing the credit cards was an important move. My story may not be the perfect example for a young reader, but if you have a parent like mine who is living with dementia, you'll see it's a good way to protect them from themselves. It's also a good way to do it for yourself.

You're reading this, so you probably don't have dementia. But you might be living with shopaholism. That credit card in the freezer will force you to live within your means. But if you're starving between paychecks because of an unexpected expense, or need to fly home to see a beloved ailing relative, the cards are there as backup. Hopefully, you will have followed some of the other advice in this book, and you'll know how to avoid thawing your cards!

THE ROAD OUT OF DEBT TOWN

When many of my clients came to me, they were, frankly, pissing in the wind. Perhaps they were paying minimum payments or more, but still using their credit cards. Most had two or three cards, all at different interest rates, and all carrying balances. A vast majority were doing their best to pay more than the minimum payment on the card with the highest interest rate, which was keeping them from buying new shoes or even food. They were indentured servants to their credit card companies. This has to stop, and I'm going to give you a money miracle.

Solvency is defined as the ability to service all your debt and pay all your bills in a given month without incurring new debt. If you aren't solvent, this won't work. You'll need to skip to the next chapter. To illustrate how to drive down this road to financial freedom, I'm going to assume you have three cards, but the principle applies whether it's one or ten.

MEET THE CARDS

To stick it to the credit card companies as quickly as possible, you're going to lose a little money to them in the beginning. Don't fret over it. You're already losing. Remember, for this to work, you MUST stop charging on all your cards. They need to all go into the freezer. If you can't do this and survive, then you need to skip to the next chapter. If you're solvent, read on.

This is one of the more complicated concepts to grasp. I've done my best to make it easy by giving names to credit cards. There might be a better way to do this, but it probably requires a whiteboard and a large classroom. So humor me.

Let's say you owe money on three credit cards. We'll call them by names and introduce them to you as eligible singles:

1. Meet Bobby Bigbalance. Bobby has little or no interest rate and a high balance. Bobby has an 8,000.00 balance and an 8% interest rate. They like long walks on the beach in exotic destinations, and treating their partner gently for as long as the interest rate lasts. One late payment and things get nasty. Bobby has plans to increase the interest rate rather drastically in a few months, and you know it. Bobby's minimum payment is $100.00.
2. Meet Mason Medium. Mason has a medium interest rate and a moderate balance. They carry a $1,000.00 balance and a 16.99% interest rate. Mason is a bit shy, and is often the last to be noticed in a room full of noisy credit cards. They like to stay home and binge streaming media on Friday nights. They

haven't been on a date in a long time. Their minimum payment is $25.00.

3. Meet Harper Hightower. Harper has a horrendously high interest rate and a massive balance. Harper is extremely outgoing and also very demanding. Even when their partner pays more than the minimum, they always seem to need more. And yet everyone seems to love Harper. They have a 29.99% interest rate, a $10,000.00 balance, and a minimum payment of $350.00. That minimum just kept climbing higher and higher. Enough is enough!

You've met them already; they've been living in your wallet or in a dresser drawer (or by now they should have moved to the freezer). They seem to get the amount of attention they ask for.

Bobby Bigbalance asks for 100 dollars, but you give them $150.00. You're hoping to get the balance down to a reasonable amount when the higher interest rate kicks in. You use Bobby for lunches and dinners out, and the occasional trip out of town.

Poor Mason just gets the minimum payment of $25.00 each month, but they seem content. They don't ask for a lot of interest, and things are pretty solid with them.

You're currently dating Harper. Harper buys you clothes, pays your bills, and pays for almost everything, really. You love Harper. Putting Harper in the freezer is extremely painful. The balance is high, and you want to pay it down, so you give them $450.00 per month, $100.00 more than the minimum. But for some reason, they just keep asking for more and more.

So let's do a little bit of math. If you add together $150.00 for Bobby Bigbalance, $25.00 for Mason Medium, and $450.00 for Harper Hightower, you get $625.00 per month. That's a lot of money you could have, but you seem to be able to pay it each month.

Traditional wisdom tells you that you need to pay Harper the most, because they're asking for the most, and charging you the most. Wrong! *Your well-being comes before your credit cards.* I'll show you how to ensure this by turning your payment strategy on its head.

Payoff Part I - Lowest balance first – Mason Medium

Like we said, you're solvent. After you stop using your credit cards, you're still able to break even or save a little. The combined total you're paying to your three cards is *$625.00* per month. I'm going to tell you to re-allocate all you can to Mason, **the sweet, simple card with the lowest balance,** no matter what their interest rate. Those other two can wait. You will pay them only the minimum.

Here's how you're going to continue to pay $625.00 per month towards your three cards, but in a different pattern:

Give Bobby the current minimum - $100.00 every month. When the minimum payment goes down, just keep giving them $100.00. Don't ask questions, and Bobby will be fine.

Lucky Mason! This shy, easygoing card used to get a measly $25.00, and now they get $175.00! They're not used to all this attention!

Harper has had too much and can learn to live with less. Give Harper the minimum $350.00 every month (even when the minimum payment amount goes down). Remember, you put Harper in the freezer and cancelled or migrated all those subscriptions, so Harper is not going to ask for more each month.

You're still paying the same amount each month, *$625.00*, but the allocations have changed.

What happens next?

In less than a year, *Mason Medium is all paid off.* Your relationship is over, but it was really for the best that it ended. Hooray, you have $175.00 per month to spare now, right? WRONG. Read on.

BEFORE

BOBBY BIGBALANCE
8.99% APR
$8,000.00 Balance
$100.00 Minimum Pay

You're
Paying
$150.00

MASON MEDIUM
16.99% APR
$1,000 Balance
$25.00 Minimum Payment

You're
Paying
$25.00

HARPER HIGHTOWER
29.99% APR
$10,000 Balance
$350.00 Minimum Payment

You're
Paying
$450.00

Total: $625
Per Month

NOW

BOBBY BIGBALANCE
8.99% APR
$8,000.00 Balance
$100.00 Minimum Pay

Just Pay
$100.00

MASON MEDIUM
16.99% APR
$1,000 Balance
$25.00 Minimum Payment

Pay
$175.00

HARPER HIGHTOWER
29.99% APR
$10,000.00 Balance
$350.00 Minimum Payment

Just Pay
$350.00

Total: $625
Per Month

ONE YEAR LATER

BOBBY BIGBALANCE
8.99% APR
$7,000.00 Balance
$90.00 Minimum Pay

Pay
$275.00

MASON MEDIUM
PAID OFF!

HARPER HIGHTOWER
29.99% APR
$9,500.00 Balance
$320.00 Minimum Payment

Keep
Paying
$350.00

Total: $625
Per Month

THREE YEARS LATER

BOBBY BIGBALANCE
PAID OFF!

MASON MEDIUM
PAID OFF!

HARPER HIGHTOWER
29.99% APR
$8,000.00 Balance
$300.00 Minimum Payment

Pay
$625.00

Will be all paid off
in 18 Months!

Total: $625
Per Month

Payoff Part II - Down to 2 cards
LOWEST BALANCE FIRST still applies.

Do you start paying more to the fussy, demanding Harper now so they'll stop charging you so much? No! Harper can wait. And they will.

You take all $175.00 that you were paying Mason and *add it to the $100.00 minimum* that you were paying Bobby Bigbalance. Now you're paying $275.00 to Bobby, and Harper gets their original minimum payment of $350.00.

Bobby was at $8,000.00 with a minimum of $100.00 when you started in Part I. After a year, they'll be at about $7,000.00 with a minimum payment of about $90.00. Here's the thing - as long as you are paying the old minimum of $350.00 to Harper and not using that card, you're paying them off! Yes, the interest is costly, but you're now in a position where you might be able, once in a while, to pay a minimum on both cards to free up a little cash. This is like an emergency budget item. Don't do it often. Bobby Bigbalance is going down rapidly. If a windfall comes in, you add some to your savings and apply most of it to Bobby to help reduce the balance even faster. But for the sake of argument, you're going to keep paying.

Note: A "windfall" is a chunk of unexpected money. Windfalls will change everything, but they are called windfalls because they blow into your life unexpectedly. You can't count on them, but they are really nice when they happen. More about Windfalls in Chapter 7.

Payoff Part III - Just Harper now!

The numbers are REALLY hard to calculate, and they'll make your head spin, but let's just say that over the course of 3 years, you have paid down Bobby to $0.00, and Harper is now at around $8,000.00.

You're going to now take all $625.00 and apply it to Harper. What? Can't I have a little for myself, you ask? Well, maybe, but by now you've had a raise, some side income, and other things that have made this whole re-payment scheme a lot easier. With $625.00 going to-wards the $8,000.00, you'll see a drastic reduction in your balance each month. Your credit score has sky-rocketed as a result of paying off the other two.

Sidebar – Lou Low
Credit card companies are DYING to give you a new card, and will bait you with a tempting 21 months at 0% interest balance transfer offers. I say, take the bait. What? It's not a trick?

You kiss Harper goodbye and move on to your new friend, Lou Low. Yes, you'll get hit with about 3% in im-mediate interest. Your balance creeps up slightly. Let's say it goes up $250.00. But the savings from 29.99% compound interest are insanely good. Now, each time you pay $625.00, your balance decreases by $625.00! Your card is paid off in less than two years. And NOW you're wealthy. Seriously. You suddenly have an extra $625.00 a month to drop into an emergency savings ac-count or, better yet, a nice blended mutual fund.

Even if you never get an offer from Lou Low, this whole thing could take less than four years, and you've come out smelling like roses. AND you didn't have to add any more to the total amount of $625.00 that you were already paying towards the cards.

This was one example, but the same principles ap-ply. Always pay extra towards the card with the lowest balance and the minimum payment on all others. When it's done, add the entire amount to the next card. It costs a little more, but it gets you out of debt faster!

ALL PAID OFF - NOW WHAT?

Once you have zero balances, it is not an invitation to drive your balances back up. I strongly recommend continuing to use debit for many months as you get used to the feeling of having zero debt. It's freeing. You may have lived with a debt addiction, and you're detoxing now.

Here's some bad news: some of you will never be able to use credit cards like a normal person. You'll find excuses to avoid paying your balance in full, and you'll be back in the trap that every bank hopes you will fall for. Debt is a drug. Shopping is a drug. Underearning is a drug. It's all drugs! So be very careful before you begin using credit cards responsibly, or you might get strung out.

RESPONSIBLE DEBTING

Here's how you use credit cards responsibly. It's simple. Pay down your balance to zero several times a month. Never carry a balance for longer than a month. I challenge you, after six months clean from debt, to use your best credit card (with the best cash-back deal) for a few purchases. Pay off the balance in full before the next bill is due. Do this for two months. If you still have a zero balance at the end of that period, repeat the process for another two months. Has the habit of paying it off kicked in, or are you back to your old habits?

If you've learned how to pay in full, and you're still at zero balance each month, then it's time to start moving your bills and other monthly expenses to a cash-back credit card.

If instead you didn't pay it in time, and you've carried a balance long enough to get hit with interest charges, then I'm sorry, you'll need another six months of debt abstinence before you try again. You may need to use a debit card for the rest of your life. However, hopefully, the good habits you've built over those two-month increments will prove that you have the discipline to use a credit card responsibly. It's different for each person, case by case. Be honest with yourself and act accordingly.

INSOLVENCY

Now let's talk about what happens if you can't even pay the minimum without charging more on something else. You're insolvent. What does that mean? It means you've dug a hole so deep, you won't be able to get out.

TAKING A CREDIT CARD VACATION

Insolvent? Take a break, and don't pay. It's a vacation from financial stress. Maybe a permanent one!

What? What's that? It's simple. Stop paying the damn cards. Just stop. Does your livelihood and well-being come before the credit card company's well-being? NO. Is your credit score important? YES. Is it screwed forever if you do this? NO.

Credit scores are what my husband's father used to refer to as "tu record." He'd say, "Cuida tu record, mijo." (Take care of your record, son.). Yes, we all want to be model citizens and take part in society. But we may have screwed up and need to fix it.

I probably need a lawyer to write this disclaimer, but here's what I want you to understand. This will mess with your credit score. If you need a new car, you may need to wait and take the bus for a while. If you want to buy a house, you have to wait.

Let me also tell you this: I took a credit vacation, and I bought a car WHILE I was doing it. I bought a house about seven years after it was over. It may be a sad turn of events, but it will have a happy ending.

A Secret…shh!

This is not a dirty little secret. This is a HUGE FILTHY SECRET that credit card companies don't want you to know: You don't owe them a goddamn thing. They trusted you and you trusted them…but they screwed you up in return for your trust in them. They WANT your money, but it's up to you to give it to them. If you're not able to live without charging more, STOP PAYING.

It may only take a few months to get back on track. Maybe you get a raise at work or find a side hustle that pays really well (more about Side Hustles in Chapter 6. The banks are going to light up your phone morning, noon and night. Take their calls now and then and tell them you've had a major setback. They've lied to you, so you can lie right back. Tell them you're having a medical crisis and need six months to get back on your feet. I did something like this with the largest bank in the US. As I've mentioned, I have lived my whole adult life with a well-treated but serious psychiatric illness. When I told that lady at the bank that I was dealing with a medical crisis, it was true. Furthermore, every day that goes by where you can't afford your health insurance and medicine is a medical crisis.

What happens? A few things happen. The first month that you don't pay, you suddenly have more money in your budget. Your credit score begins to nosedive. This is a perfect time to buy a cheap used car if you can afford the payments. You'll get a sucky interest rate, but you'll have extra cash to pay the higher car payments. Remember, a car is secured debt. Unlike credit cards, a car can be repossessed. Repossession is when the tow truck shows up and hauls away your car. More dings to your credit score, but it means you're off the hook for whatever you didn't pay. You don't owe any more. I think a car dealership may put a hit out on me if they read this, so if I die mysteriously, you'll know why.

In the second month of your credit vacation, you have that extra money, and you'll be getting letters, phone calls, and nasty emails from your cards. So what? You'll pay them when you're good and ready.

In month three, things start to reach a fever point. Your credit score has plummeted, you get bombarded by the banks. So what?

What is the worst that can happen?

Some banks just give up and ding your credit score as hard as they can. When it's a significant amount that is owed, some try to levy a judgment against you and force you to go to court. That's the worst-case scenario. It didn't happen to me. But even if it had, after that, I would have had a no-interest structured payment plan tailored to prevent me from going hungry, and my credit score would not have been affected any further.

It takes seven years for your credit score to bounce back completely from a credit card permanent vacation. It takes about five years if you come back from vacation and pay them off. Your "record" isn't permanent. It heals itself once the crisis is over. And, in the meantime, your budget is freed up to save, and you can move on to the next chapter.

MONEY MIRACLE

A CREDIT CARD VACATION

In my 30s, I took a credit card vacation. I stopped paying credit cards and started socking away as much of the extra cash as I could. One credit card company sent me a letter saying that they would be willing to forgive all the interest and take a payment that was about 1/10 of the outstanding balance. I paid them. What the hell? I'd saved some money, and I could get one of those bastards off my back. Then I finally sold a documentary film I'd made during the time I was racking up all the debt. I called the remaining three banks and told them I was ready to pay up, but I needed a break on the total. They all agreed to take what I could give them. They drove my credit score into the ground, but then it was over.

What would have happened if I hadn't come into an unexpected chunk of change? I can't say for sure, but it probably would have ended with all the banks agreeing to settle for less.

REWARDS POINTS - A SHELL GAME

I see that hand raised in the back of the room. One of you asks, "But what about rewards points and cash back? Debit cards don't have them."

No, they don't.

A shell game is a confidence trick where a dealer hides a ball under one of three covers (shells), shuffles them, and players bet on its location. Sleight of hand typically favors the dealer. With rewards points, the dealer always wins. *Unless* you are debt-free and paying off the balance every month. In that case, the dealer loses.

Until you have carried a zero balance for multiple months and know you can maintain a zero balance, rewards points will be a con game in light of compound interest. What's 1% cash back if you're paying 25% on the entire total? You owe $8,000.00. If you spend $1,000.00 each month and pay just $800.00, you get $10.00 cash back that month. And now you owe $8,200.00 plus interest! See how you lose?

Compare this to the situation where your balance is zero, and has been so for many months. Then you can start using a credit card with rewards points. However, you must be absolutely certain that you will pay the entire card balance before the end of each cycle. Then, and only then, will rewards points become a genuine way of building wealth.

TAKEAWAYS

- If you're actively paying down your cards, shuffle the payment so you're paying the most to the card with the lowest balance.
- When your cards are all paid off, and you keep them at zero, only then can you start using rewards points and cash back.
- If your card payments are so high that they prevent you from securing even the most basic needs, you're insolvent; take a vacation from paying them.

CHAPTER 4
THE TEN PERCENT FACTOR

TEN PERCENT OF ALL YOU EARN IS YOURS TO KEEP

The foundation of all economic security is building savings and cultivating an investing habit. The wisdom of the ages states that ten percent of all you earn is yours to KEEP.

The first time I heard this, I honestly heard that it was mine to SPEND. You can't spend your money and keep it, too! To keep means to save. To keep means to invest. It does NOT mean to spend. It isn't for necessities of the moment, and it isn't to buy shiny things. The 10% you set aside is for your future and to build a rainy day fund. That's it! You set aside ten percent of your after-tax earnings.

Why do you do this? There are two reasons.

The First Reason - Emergency Fund

First, you need to prepare for an emergency. You may find you've lost your job, or you have unexpected medical expenses. In that situation, you need cash on hand to pay your bills and keep food on the table. The emergency fund should be at least enough to live on for three months if nothing else were coming in. Always set aside money for this until you've reached at least three months' worth of living expenses (rent, food, utilities). Once you have done so, you can save for the second reason.

The Second Reason - Wealth For The Future

Savings is the foundation of wealth. When you have any amount of money earning interest or dividends, you're generating wealth. Most interest rates on savings accounts are abysmally low, but even a penny in interest (which one of my accounts earns on a bimonthly basis) is wealth. As of this writing, you can find savings accounts that pay 4-5% annual interest. Those generate a lot more than a penny, even on a small amount.

I know your first question. "But how can I save when I can barely make ends meet?"

The answer is simple: you adjust what you mean by making ends meet. I have a money miracle for you that makes this a lot easier.

MONEY MIRACLE

'AUTOMAGIC' SAVINGS

If you have direct deposit at work, this is the easiest way to build this ten-percent habit. You start off easy with one percent. If your take-home pay for two weeks is $1,200.00, you would arrange with HR or your payroll provider to have $12.00 of that deposited in your savings account instead of your checking. It's painless. You won't even notice it. Once you're comfortable that you won't go hungry, move it up to five percent. That would be $60.00. Eventually, you're going to find it's easy to go up another few percentage points, maybe all the way to $120.00 per paycheck. The beauty is that you don't have to lift a finger and the savings just pour in.

PROTECTING YOUR FUTURE

"But wait," you say, "Aren't I supposed to be putting money in my 401(k)?" The short answer is, "Yes, of course." But not so much that you end up having to re-sort to a credit card to cover your basic expenses. Saving for the future means nothing if you're incurring debt in the present and unable to put any portion of your money aside. But I said yes, so let's unpack this.

There are two kinds of savings. There are the au-tomagic savings I described in the Money Miracle, which generate money on hand for emergencies and eventually for investing. But there are also the savings for the future, tax-protected investments. Let's talk about this second kind now.

TAX-PROTECTED RETIREMENT SAVINGS – 401(K)S AND IRAS

Warning! This retirement section may be incredibly boring, but it's important.

Your paycheck is your money to do with in a manner that sustains you now and in the future. Esti-mates indicate that approximately 60% of employees in the US are eligible for a 401(k) plan. Of those employ-ees, about two-thirds make use of them, which is great.

If you're at a workplace with a 401(k) plan and you're not using it, you're throwing away free money. Here's why.

First, a traditional 401(k) plan lets you put off paying income tax on money you're earning now. So when you put $100.00 into a 401(k), you pay a little less in taxes in the present moment. So it's a little bit of free money. If you defer $100.00 now, your paycheck will only feel like you've set aside $80.00. It isn't truly free, because you have to pay those taxes later, in retirement, when you withdraw the money from the account. This is different from a Roth 401(k), which I'll explain later.

The real free money often comes from your employer. Many 401(k) plans include employer matching contributions. That means for every dollar you contribute, they will contribute some money as well. I've had generous employers who matched dollar for dollar up to 10% of my income. So, in a simple example, if I made $1,000.00/month and put in $100.00/month, they would put in $100.00/month. *That's completely free money!*

I had an extremely ungenerous employer who agreed to match 5% of my contributions, up to 1% of my income. So, if I make $1,000.00 per month and put in $100.00, the employer would put in $5.00. The most they'd put in would be $10.00! That stinks. But it's FREE MONEY all the same. True, you can't touch it until you're nearly 60 years old, but it's free, and you should squeeze every penny you can out of your employer.

Until I was in my thirties, I didn't understand how 401(k)s worked, so I blew them off. Don't do that, please! Employer matching is one type of free money, but there's another.

Normally, when you sell stock for more than you paid, you owe taxes on it. They call it "Capital Gains Tax".

Capital gains in a traditional 401(k) plan **are not taxable**. So if you double your money in the market (your stocks are worth twice what you paid), you won't owe taxes on that doubling. You WILL owe employment (payroll) taxes in a traditional 401(k) retirement account at the time you withdraw the money, but you won't have to pay capital gains on top of that.

This brings me to the Roth account. These are different. Your employer may offer a Roth 401(k). This is a lot more like a savings account. You don't receive a tax break on your paycheck for contributing money to a

Roth. You'll even incur payroll taxes on what your employer matches. But you only pay those payroll taxes once. Just like a 401(k), the capital gains are tax-free. So unlike a traditional 401(k), at retirement, you will pay **no taxes whatsoever** when you withdraw the money. It's all yours. So why wouldn't you do a Roth? Remember, I said they tax your earnings with a Roth. So your paycheck is smaller. It's a question of paying taxes now or paying them later. If you're in a cash crunch, a traditional (non-Roth) 401(k) is a way to save without breaking your budget. You'll pay those taxes when you reach retirement age and start withdrawing from the account.

If you're self-employed or your employer offers no 401(k) plan, you can still set up a retirement account. You can reach out to a financial services firm (a financial advisor) and ask if they'll take you on as a client. These accounts, which you fund yourself, are called Individual Retirement Accounts (IRAs). There's a traditional and a Roth IRA available to you, and the taxes work the same. Your traditional IRA will save you on income taxes now, and the Roth will save you later.

These are the best ways to save for the distant future. But you have an obligation to yourself in the present to have an emergency fund. This is a savings account.

If your eyes glazed over during this last section, you're probably not alone. I found this stuff incredibly boring. It was about the distant future during a time when my present moment was all about scarcity. Just promise me that you'll return to this retirement section and re-read it once every few weeks until it makes sense! Your employer may not thank me for explaining it, as it costs them money, but don't be one of the many workers and earners who are not saving for their future. Read this, ask AI, do whatever it takes to understand retirement plans and how they work. Or you can try this Money Miracle.

MONEY MIRACLE

ASKING AI

Artificial Intelligence is great at explaining complex concepts. As a writer, I don't like to use it in my writing because it will learn from me and put me out of a job someday. Nonetheless, I'd recommend asking exactly the following question of Chat GPT, Google Gemini, or your favorite AI:

"I'm new to personal finance, and I would like to understand retirement savings better. Can you explain and point out the differences between Roth IRAs, Traditional IRAs, Roth 401(k)s and Traditional 401(k)s? Please detail the tax implications for each of the four types."

. . .

Okay, enough about saving. Let's talk about spending!

CHAPTER 5
SPENDING PLANS

We've used an app to find and classify your expenses each month. In the process, we've discovered several interesting ways you're losing money each month. This is the chapter where we double down on those expenses and build a spending plan.

There is a subtle difference between a budget and a spending plan. A budget approaches your money with a scarcity mentality. It asks you to slash and burn all seemingly unnecessary expenses. It says what you CAN'T do, not what you can. If there's anything left over, that either gets snatched up into a miserly savings plan, or, if you're really good, you can have a guilty pleasure or two. It's designed to help you achieve balance between your earnings, savings, and spending. It works, but it can be painful. I need you to be brave.

A spending plan accomplishes the same thing, but it's written backwards. You start with the things you love and can't do without. Rather than taking your rent, food, utilities, credit card bills, and savings and subtracting them from your income, you back into those things.

To get started, take out two pieces of paper. Label one "Passions" and the other one "Spending Plan". At the top of the Spending Plan, put your monthly income.

Remember, if you are paid every week or every two weeks, for instance, you should add up all your paychecks for a year and divide by 12.

Below that, put one wide column labeled "Item", one narrow column labeled "Monthly Cost", and a column of checkboxes labeled "Discretionary?"

Multiply the income by 10% to determine your savings line item, which MUST come before any other expenses are even considered. Subtract that to get your after-savings income. You bring home $5,000.00 a month after taxes? Put down $500.00 under savings. Your after-savings income is $3,500.00. Use this figure for all your subsequent calculations. See the figure for an example.

SPENDING PLAN

Annual Take Home Income: $36,000.00 After Taxes
Monthly Take-Home: $3,000.00

CATEGORY	AMOUNT
Savings	$3,000.00 x 10% = $300.00 Leaves $2,700
Rent	-$1,800.00 Leaves $900
Groceries	-$100.00 Leaves $800
Credit Cards	-$625.00 Leaves $175
Subscriptions	-$40.00 Leaves $135
Utilities	-$90 Leaves $45
Dining	-$200 Leaves -$155

On the Passions page, jot down all the things you love to do in your free time. They can be anything - going to lunch with colleagues, getting your nails done, hang gliding, horseback riding, international travel…it doesn't matter, just write down all the things you'd do if you had the money. These are your passions.

Think about your passions. Some of them cost almost nothing. I love to write. It doesn't cost me more than an annual subscription to Microsoft Word. If I use Google Docs, it's completely free. Put a big star next to these types of tiny expenses on your list. Determine their monthly cost and record it on the Spending Plan page. If you live near the coast, swimming in the ocean might be the cost of a bus ride or gas. If you love to sing or play music, it's often free or cheap. Good. Add the minuscule cost to your spending plan, and don't mark it as discretionary. Consider these mandatory, non-discretionary expenses. They are tiny expenses that will enrich your life.

But let's say your deepest passion is expensive. Maybe you like to go to a concert every month. Tickets are really expensive. You might be looking at $300.00 a month or more. My expensive passion is fine dining. I like to have one expensive meal a month at a nice restaurant. That might be $300.00 per month. Maybe it's the aforementioned hang gliding or international travel. Whatever it is, jot it down on the Passions page and calculate the expense, breaking it down to a monthly average.

Put these costlier passions on your Spending Plan, but be sure to tick the "discretionary" box.

On the Spending Plan, you now add some basic living expenses that are basically fixed and unavoidable. These are housing, insurance, health care, income taxes, groceries, utilities, transportation, gas,

Next, consult the finance app to determine how much you spend annually on restaurants, entertainment, clothing, gym/exercise, and gifts. Divide by twelve months and add these to the spending plan, but mark them as discretionary.

This usually leaves no more than 10% unaccounted for. You can dig down in the app to see what else is there, or you can take that remaining amount and call it "Miscellaneous." Some of the things that take a little research are usually found by drilling down into that thin sliver on the pie chart of your expenses. There will be some stuff there where you say to yourself, "What the hell is that?"

Home
Utilities
Groceries
Dining
→ Everything Else

INVESTIGATE TILL YOU KNOW WHAT <u>EVERYTHING ELSE</u> IS

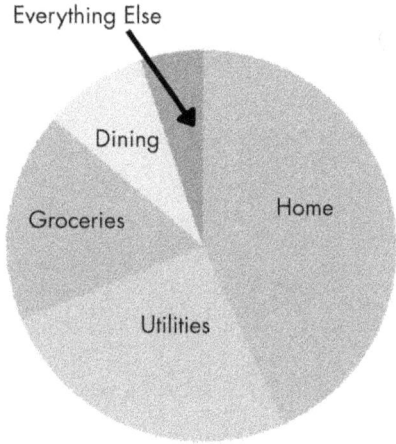

Everything Else

Dining

Groceries

Home

Utilities

I recommend investigating until you reach the point that Miscellaneous or 'Everything Else' is no more than 5%. As you'll see, the more you know, the more wiggle room you'll have in the next part of this exercise.

If you're any good at Excel, I recommend transferring your Spending plan to an Excel workbook. Or Google Sheets. If not, a calculator will work fine.

Start with the non-discretionary items. Add all the monthly non-discretionary costs, and subtract that from your after-savings monthly income. It's pretty likely that you'll still have a positive number. If you don't, you're in trouble. You'll need to skip to the chapter about underearning and side hustles and return once you've performed a few miracles from there.

If the number is still positive, then add in the most dreadful part - credit cards. The one thing I haven't discussed is credit card payments. The minimum payments on each card create a line in the spending plan, but you will mark it as discretionary. We already know that paying off credit cards is a luxury you might not be able to afford! At this point, the number on your calculator/spreadsheet is probably negative, but maybe not. Keep going for now, because we need to know just how negative it is!

MONEY MIRACLE

ASYMMETRY IN SPENDING

Before we delve into the details of the spending plan, I'd like to introduce a concept that will really help you. There is a phenomenon in a spending plan where certain expenses, when increased, can disproportionately lower other expenses. The best example is groceries and restaurants. If you spend an additional $100.00 on groceries, it will reduce your restaurant spending by $200.00. It only works if you actually cook the groceries, of course. There is a strange exception where dining out actually doesn't change things: In the case of really unhealthy fast food restaurants, they cost about the same as groceries, perhaps even less. These dealers in early death employed economies of scale such that it costs just about the same to have a cheap burger and fries as it would to cook at home. Many people have learned to go to fast food restaurants instead of cooking. That's how they've managed to poison us. But I digress.

Other areas where you might notice this asymmetry include thrift shopping versus clothes shopping. You can spend $25.00 at a thrift store and avoid $100.00

worth of clothes shopping. If sewing is one of your passions, you can increase your sewing budget and see a drastic drop in your clothing budget as well. If you buy a bag of incredible coffee for $20.00 and commit to making it for yourself, your coffee shop expenses will drop drastically. If running is a passion, and the gym isn't, then investing in good running shoes could do away with your gym expenses altogether! I would even go so far as to say that in summertime, you can increase your beachgoing expenses and see a larger drop in your utility bills because your A/C will be off! See if you can think of some other examples of asymmetry in your expenses.

———————

. . .

Locking In Your Spending Plan

You now have a number, which is the difference between your monthly after-savings income and your non-discretionary expenses. It's probably a lot smaller than you hoped. If it's negative, you're experiencing a financial emergency! You'll need to take a credit card vacation or get a side hustle as explained in Chapter 6. But assuming it's a positive amount, we're going to make this work. We'll call it the discretionary fund.

You'll be doing a lot of adjusting here, so if you're not using Excel or Google Sheets with a formula, I recommend doing this next part in pencil so you can make changes.

Look at each of the discretionary expense categories you identified - restaurants, entertainment, clothing, gym/exercise, and gifts, plus any others that you found digging deeper in your app. When you subtract all of these from the discretionary, I am nearly certain that you'll see a negative number. (If you don't, then you're only reading this book because you're considering it as a gift!) Fixing this negative number is precisely why this book exists. We're about to fix it.

To start, don't trim anything that came from your passions page. Not even the expensive stuff. You may need to revisit them, but maybe not. Cross that bridge when you get to it.

Let's start with restaurants. I've explained in the Money Miracle how to lower that number through the magic of asymmetry. It's a guess, but increasing your monthly grocery expenses by $100.00 should allow you to lower your restaurant expenses by $200.00. Use that rule of thumb. You must commit to cooking more. I'll begrudgingly add that you can occasionally skip cooking and opt for fast food a few times, using money from your grocery budget rather than your restaurant budget. I hate it, but it's true. Don't make it a habit. And if restaurant dining is a passion, make sure to revisit it when we're examining the discretionary passions.

Entertainment expenses can vary wildly. Going to the movies costs a lot less than going to a live arena concert. Almost every home has subscriptions to entertainment platforms - movies, games, etc. Some gamers spend hundreds a month. I spend ten dollars on Apple News for the crossword puzzles. If your number for entertainment is already low, you may not be able to do much besides eliminating some entertainment that you can do without. I dump streaming platforms and periodically subscribe back to them for a month to binge on the shows I missed. It saves me around $75.00 a month, and I still have the two main platforms I use the most. Definitely review your entertainment subscriptions and see where you can make some cuts. Live sports, music, and shows are often on someone's passions list. We need to be sure you aren't double-counting those. I don't like baseball. Maybe you don't much either, but you have a friend who insists every year that you go in on season tickets. This will be the year you tell that friend no. The way to look at Entertainment, which is at the heart of so many passions, is to see what you need all the time to feel alive and move that over to passions. The rest you may need to forgo or drastically reduce. One movie premiere a month instead of three. Three great concerts a year instead of twenty. You get the idea.

Clothing is a wild card. I have clients who spend almost nothing on clothing, and others who were in the poor house for clothing expenses alone! If shopping for luxury clothes is on your passion list, then it is discretionary. Remove any clothing expenses from non-discretionary and skip down to the passions portion. If you are somewhere between nothing and thousands for clothing, consider the asymmetry of thrift shopping as one way to drastically reduce your clothing expenses without sacrificing comfort. If you aren't an experienced thrifter, here's a tip: it's best to go thrifting in expensive neighborhoods. Thrifters who count it as a passion will already know where to find the bargains.

Exercise is not a luxury. I was a couch potato for far too much of my life, and I'm paying the price now. I work out every day now, but it's not easy. If I had made it a habit and stuck with it, I'd probably have added ten years to my life expectancy. So when we call the gym a discretionary expense, it's more about the price. I work out at a crappy gym near my house. The sauna is filled with men who haven't meditated a day in their life. They feel compelled to blabber on and fill the quiet space with their voices. Still, there's a sauna. The equipment allows me to do my daily routine. It's good enough. I'd love to be at a nicer place, but the proximity to my house, two blocks, is almost unheard of in Los Angeles, a city where you drive for 20 minutes to do almost everything. So I go to the crappy gym and put up with the yapping assholes in the sauna.

If you live for bodybuilding, then the gym expense should show up as a passion. Otherwise, it's here as discretionary for a reason. You may be paying country club prices for a gym when you can pay just $25.00 a month, or nothing at all. Be honest with yourself. Do you need a gym with chilled cucumber water and L'Occitane soap dispensers? Is that the only way you'll ever work out? Do you get most of your exercise in a home gym anyway?

What I hope to impress upon you is that exercise is a necessary activity, but where you do it is not always a necessary expense. If you conduct all your business deals at a high-end gym and it improves your bottom line, the expense is worth it. If you only ever see friends at a particular class at the expensive gym, and you would have to give that up, it might be worth it, but it might be cheaper to have a book club and rope them all in. Think about it. How important is the quality of the gym versus its impact on your spending for the month?

Can you sacrifice and still take excellent care of your health?

GIFTS

Here's a touchy subject. Some of my clients spend hundreds of dollars a month on gifts because so many of their friends are getting married at this point in their lives. Gifts are wonderful. They can mean so much. But that isn't limited to a positive meaning. Some gifts say, "See, I'm doing better than you." Are you giving from your heart, or is the gift a disguise to cover up financial reality? It's a terrible question, but you need to ask it of yourself. Can you spend a long time thinking about a person and give them a ten-dollar gift that would brighten their day?

I volunteer at a museum. One employee there has helped me by putting my books in the gift store. I wanted to show my appreciation. A box of items came in, and she wandered around, cursing her fellow employees because they were forever taking her box cutter. She ended up using a butter knife to cut the plastic straps. While she was doing that, I was on Amazon looking at box cutters. I found a red one for $9.00 and sent it to her while she was talking to me and complaining! My gift note said, "Now you can catch those thieves red-handed!" That's how you give a gift. Make it simple and meaningful.

Conversely, you may have spent nothing on gifts due to being in scarcity mode. I have had those years. What's important is to have strength of purpose in your gift-giving. Have clear, graceful intentions. Don't equate price or labels with quality. That box cutter is probably one of my friend's favorite items at work now. You don't have to spend a fortune, but you should spend a little something here and there. That's why we call it a spending plan.

After gifts, it's time to look at credit card bills. Damn those credit cards! Let's discuss a money miracle that can help a little with getting your spending plan back on track. This assumes you stopped using the little bug-gers and stuck them in the freezer. If you haven't, then this miracle (and perhaps this book) isn't for you!

MONEY MIRACLE

BALANCE TRANSFERS

Balance transfers seem too good to be true. Why would a bank offer 0% interest for 12-18 months? What's in it for them? Easy. They take a flat 3% of your transfer amount and pocket it. Plus, they're gambling that you won't be all paid up after the grace period expires, so then they get to start collecting an exorbitant 29.99% annual interest. It's a trap! Oh no! But you can use it to your advantage.

I'm never one for encouraging you to give 3% of your money away, but what if it buys you some breathing room? Your minimum monthly payment plummets when you transfer your balance from an interest-bearing card to a zero-interest card. That results in a significant reduction in the line items of your spending plan. So, consider a balance transfer if you can get one. Transfer all your balances if you can. It's best to have a single card. By the time the grace period is up, you'll have a dozen more cards offering you the same deal. However, remember that it costs money each time you do a balance transfer. You don't feel the expense, but it shows up in your debt balance on the card.

. . .

ARE WE POSITIVE YET?

If you have credit card debt, it's likely that you still haven't reached a positive number after these exercises. After subtracting ten percent savings, non-discretionary expenses, discretionary expenses, and credit card bills from your net income, you're still at a negative number.

Here is where you have to get creative. First, protect the three essential spending categories: your savings, your affordable passions, and your non-discretionary expenses. If you're still at a negative balance, skip to Chapter 6, which discusses underearning.

If you're positive, but even after a balance transfer, your minimum credit card payments put you into the negative, then it's time for that money miracle I called "A Credit Card Vacation."

If you are able, make your minimum credit card payments, which is preferable to f*ing up your credit.

Looking at your discretionary passion-based expenses, you prioritize them. You can live without any of them, but which can you live without the least? When you remove all of them from your plan, you should see a positive number. Again, if you aren't in the black, meaning you have a positive number, you need Chapter 6 to help you.

Keep the first one. Is it clothing? Is it the gym? Whatever it is, keep it, and see if you're in the red or in the black. At the risk of over-explaining, red and black are accounting terms. Red indicates a negative value, while black represents a positive value. Next, include the next discretionary expense and subtract its cost from the total. Are you still positive? Continue until you turn negative, then apply these miracle cures to the rest:

Austerity Without Temerity

You can cut expenses without completely sacrificing

your quality of life. You are likely at a point in your life where your expenses exceed your income. Here are some tricks and tips to keep you going at no cost while you continue to work some of the miracles in this book and achieve prosperity.

Restaurants: You need to stop eating out and cook at home. Just do it. From your grocery expenses, you may splurge on some 10-dollar meals from a fast food joint or a food truck. Have a mini-potluck with a couple of friends, where each of you cooks simple food for the others. Casseroles and stews keep well. Plan more plant-based meals that cost a lot less than meat and dairy.

Entertainment: - Cancel paid platforms and watch on the free apps. Stop going to the movies - wait for it to come to your library or another free platform. Don't pay for concerts; there are plenty of great bands who'd love you to come see them for free! Change how you watch sporting events. Watch on free TV (not ESPN), attend minor league games, or simply sit and watch the guys play hoops. Get creative with how you entertain yourself.

Clothing: Go thrifting if you can afford it. If you can't, just wear the same clothes until after you've worked some more money miracles. Go to clothing exchanges where friends swap clothing. Sew your buttons back on instead of throwing the item away.

Gym/Exercise: Work out at a park near you that has one of those outdoor gyms. Go running and hiking. Walk to work. Take the stairs at work. Do Tai Chi in the park. There are many ways to exercise besides going to the gym. Even libraries have exercise programs! And if you're in school, the gym is usually available for free.

Gifts: Make your own. Make a card. Write a poem or short story about the person. Give a warm, welcome hug. Go for a walk together.

. . .

Cutting the Seemingly Uncuttable

Non-discretionary expenses appear fixed and immovable, but there are ways to reduce them. Some have far more impact than others. Turning the heat down in the winter will likely increase your medical expenses, so don't try that one!

Housing: Moving is a significant expense, but consider subletting a room to someone. There are plenty of people who only need a room for one or two nights a week, for instance. Can you manage a roommate, or is your place too small?

Phone and Internet: Bundle and save. Find a provider who charges less than what you're paying. Bundles are the most common example of this. Ask a lot of questions and seek online opinions before making any switch. These providers are skilled at deceiving you, so read the fine print carefully. I successfully merged my cable internet and phone services, saving over $100.00 per month. So check that one out. I know the cost increases after a year, but it's a great cost-saving measure in the short term, and maybe even in the long run. And it may never be as expensive as what you were paying before!

Groceries: Grocery stores come in tiers. At the top are the luxury grocers: Whole Foods, Gelsons, Bi-Rite, and Zabar's, to name a few. If you're shopping there, it's time to tighten the belt. You can drop down one tier to the Kroger/Safeway/Piggly Wiggly level, or you can go deeper, into Trader Joe's territory. You can even go deeper to get rock-bottom prices at Food 4 Less and Walmart. You can pay $30.00 for an heirloom tomato salad, or you can pay $3.00 for a farm-fresh tomato salad. Shop wisely. And don't toss the circulars that come in the mail. Use them to plan a menu for the week, taking advantage of coupons and being aware of what's on sale.

Transportation: Gasoline, Uber, and Taxis: Take the bus. Don't drive to the corner store. Walk. Dust off your bicycle and enjoy the new bike lanes that are popping up everywhere. These are sort of obvious, but it bears repeating. Public transportation is way cheaper than driving. And walking is free. Ride-share apps didn't exist until recently. Like taxis before them, I only use them when the situation requires it. If I'm stranded, my life is in danger, or my ride home is drunk, then a taxi/ride share is not optional. I've taken the bus to the airport when I was broke, so you can, too.

Health Insurance: Don't mess with this one! Health insurance comes in tiers, so it's possible to drop down a tier, but it might come back to bite you in the butt if you're living with any sort of health condition. You can definitely shop around for better car insurance rates, but when you are a homeowner, or you've grown wealthy, with something to lose, don't cut corners with insurance.

These austerity measures are what we try to avoid in spending plans, but they become necessary when you're upside down, meaning that you're unable to spend less than you earn. If you want to get out from under this austerity, don't thaw a credit card, because that's only digging a deeper hole. Instead, find ways to increase your earnings. That's what we'll talk about in this next segment.

CHAPTER 6

UNDEREARNING, SIDE HUSTLES AND GIGS

WHAT IS UNDEREARNING?

Underearning is a state of not having enough. It's a constellation of behavioral symptoms and habits that cause a person to have less than they need, despite efforts to the contrary. No two under-earners are exactly alike, but they share a number of common symptoms.

If you:

- Procrastinate
- Deflect good ideas
- Feel a compulsive need to prove your worth
- Hoard possessions
- Overwork yourself to exhaustion then work too little
- Give away your time
- Undervalue your work and yourself
- Work alone when you would be better off working with the help of others
- Feel guilty or uneasy asking for what you need
- Fail to follow up on opportunities and job leads

- And/or get bored and cause problems that get you in trouble at work…

Then you might be an underearner.

Underearning is making less than you need to thrive. It's different from consciously working for less in a job that pays enough but also feeds your soul. It's not the same as being committed to living a simpler, saner life. It's never a conscious choice. You can learn a lot about it by asking an AI, "What is underearning?" Visit the Underearners Anonymous website. If you can't make ends meet and live beyond your means, or you aren't earning enough to ensure your present and future well-being, then you're underearning.

I was raised by underearners and spent the majority of my adult life as an underearner. I don't experience most of the symptoms today, but I have had nearly all of them during the course of my life. I maintain vigilance to ensure I don't regress to this state of poverty consciousness that pervaded my life. I don't know if nearly everyone has these issues or if it's just a few of us. I've definitely met people who possess an extraordinary ability to make money rain from the sky and genuinely enjoy doing it. I had an umbrella deflecting any ideas or money opportunities that came my way. I didn't think what I did was worth anything. I was afraid to change jobs and stayed stuck in some hellholes until they fired me.

You may see yourself reflected in some of the symptoms above. Here's a Money Miracle to help you. It's more of a story than a miracle, but it contains the seed of the cure to underearning.

MONEY MIRACLE

PIPE CLEANER BIRDS

A very creative and talented friend of mine took a home-based job making Christmas ornaments out of pipe cleaners. The company sent her supplies and paid her by the piece. She had other gigs, and this was just something she did sitting at home. She worked hard at it, foregoing some of her other hobbies to earn extra money. But she complained about it to me.

She said, "It's weird, I feel like I'm not making any money."
I asked, "How much do they pay you?"
She replied, "It's 15 cents per ornament."
That sounded suspicious. "How many ornaments can you make in an hour?"
She said, "I don't know. Like maybe three?"
I nearly choked. "They're paying you 45 cents an hour! You need to give that job to someone in a developing country, where they can buy a chicken with that money!"

We both couldn't stop laughing. She quit that job and returned to her hobby, photography, where she was able to earn a decent amount on the side.

———————

Why Do We Underearn?

The reasons for underearning are many. There is no cure, but you can help put the condition into remission by doing a few simple things:

First, you must be willing to change. You have to recognize when it's time to take contrary action - doing something that feels uncomfortable or maybe even sounds impossible.

Second, take contrary action. Instead of deflecting a suggestion, follow through on it. You don't want to ask for a raise, but you do it anyway. Explore the best ways to accomplish this. I suggest asking an AI "How do I ask for a raise?" Or maybe you raise your prices for your customers. Ask for advice from people qualified to give it.

Third, reduce expenses where it is not painful or dangerous to do so. That's covered in Chapter 5 with your spending plan. You can always increase your expenses (bit by bit) when things get better.

Fourth, earn more. Take on a side hustle that plays into your passion. Find a new job that pays twice what you're making now. Do what it takes to bring in more cash each month without overworking to the point of exhaustion. Avoid toxic productivity.

Fifth, when all else fails, attend a meeting of Underearners Anonymous and learn what they have to teach. There is a pathological component to underearning, and it can be particularly helpful to seek help from others who have overcome it. Take what you need and leave the rest.

SIDE HUSTLES

A side hustle is a job or business you start in addition to the work you already do.

If you absolutely love your corporate job and think you could stop underearning just by getting a better position there or at a competitor, then side hustles may not be your thing. One component of underearning is what we call underbeing. This is where you do work that you dislike at the expense of being who you really are. Many of you reading this book can relate, but there are also lots of happy employees who could stop underearning without underbeing by staying right where they are and finding a way to ascend the ladder at work to a position where they love what they do. There are so many different kinds of people out there, and how you "truly be yourself" is as varied and nuanced as the shades of colors at a paint store.

There are many ways to uncover the perfect side hustle or aspirational job. There are entire books devoted to finding your exact "color of your rainbow" in terms of work. If you love leading teams, your rainbow probably lands at a corporate job at the Director level or higher. The corporation must be doing something that aligns with your personal values, regardless of what they may be.

If you're a creative soul, you may be able to find a gig in an industry where you use your art or craft for good pay. Until then, you may want to start a side hustle.

I have a friend in Hollywood who is passionate about fashion. In high school, she and I used to go to a "dollar a pound" thrift store and hunt for gems. She found me some of the coolest clothes because she had such a good eye.

No surprise, when she graduated, she wanted to work in fashion. She didn't let hundreds of naysayers stand in her way as she pursued a career as a celebrity stylist. She took a low-paying assistant position with a stylist and learned the ropes. As more clients expressed a desire to work with her over other assistants, she gained a loyal customer base. Then she set out on her own. She now dresses celebrities for the Oscars. She makes a ton of money and gets free, expensive clothes from all the designers who want to work with her!

Her story is rare, but it clearly shows what determination and hard work can do to get you into a position you love. But if you are a slave to money, paying bills paycheck to paycheck, you might not be able to take a low-paid assistant job in the industry of your dreams, then find a way to network yourself into a well-paid position. Until that day arrives, the side hustle may be your best bet.

Let's go back to the thrift store. I used to LOVE the thrift store as a kid, and still do. There are so many treasures waiting to be uncovered. Nothing beats the thrill of finding the perfect thrift store, usually run by people who have no interest in antiques, vintage clothing, or whatever it is you love to find. My friend is a designer who runs a side hustle as an antiques dealer. He finds treasures at thrift stores and garage sales, then resells them online at a huge profit. Like me, he loves the thrill of the hunt. But he loves it so much that he has turned it into a lucrative side hustle.

I have another friend who is passionate about dogs. She learned that many police stations are underfunded and can't afford bulletproof jackets for their dogs. She established a charity to raise funds for outfitting these dogs with protective vests. It's a small operation, and it has become her full-time career. She has saved the lives of many canine heroes. Who knew a love of dogs could become a side hustle and then a full-blown career?

I know a college student who loves dogs, too. Her side hustle involves housesitting at homes with dogs. She earns $50.00 a night to stay at a house and care for the dog. It gives her enough to indulge her passions, such as getting tattoos and going to concerts.

I give these stories to help trigger the dreamer inside you. What dreams have you set aside in service to your creditors? What hobbies have you put on hold because you can't allow yourself the expense? What if the expense turned into a profit? That's a side hustle.

· · ·

ACTIVE VERSUS PASSIVE SIDE HUSTLES

Some side hustles are active and others are passive. Scouring thrift stores and selling your finds online is active hustling. It requires a lot of time out in the field. But if it is your passion, it can be rewarding both financially and spiritually.

I've had many side hustles over the years, but as I got older, I craved a more passive stream of income. By dedicating time to writing every night, I started self-publishing. Ebooks had just come out, and there were platforms where you could sell them. Shortly after that, print-on-demand became a reality. I didn't have to print hundreds of copies of a paperback to sell it. If someone ordered it online, a copy was printed and delivered to the buyer. Over time, I continued to write more books, and they began to sell. I'm a publisher now. The side hustle became my job.

Maybe you have the gift of gab. There are dozens of platforms for podcasters. You can pick up a used microphone on eBay and start right away. I did audiobooks of my fiction as podcasts and syndicated them through an inexpensive service. I did it to promote my books, so they haven't generated income. However, if you opt for the talk show route, secure the right guests, and focus on a narrow topic with an enthusiastic following, you can grow, attract advertising and sponsorships, and ultimately make it a career.

MAKING MUSIC

Whether it's small-time DJ gigs at events or a concert at a huge arena, there is money to be made in music. With apps like Garage Band and Pro Tools, even a novice can make a sonic masterpiece. They're easy to learn if you have the knack, and there are dozens of platforms where you can sell your music. If you are an avid listener, you'd be surprised how easy it is to become a creator. I started a band and made a nice chunk of change playing around town in Los Angeles. It wasn't a full-time career. My bandmates didn't want that, so we parted ways. I was disillusioned and walked away from music. I still create tracks for musicians here and around the world, using a decent microphone and GarageBand. I play an autoharp, which is a bizarre-sounding instrument with a certain appeal. I don't make much money because I don't do it much. But if you have the time and energy, it can be a great side hustle and maybe even a career.

I know jack about earning money through social media platforms, but apparently it's out there. The formula I was given is "like, follow, comment" to grow your followers. The thing is, I suck at it. You're probably better than me at it! So if you know how to get followers, do it. Just don't die doing the latest idiotic challenge!

Speaking of dying, there are some side hustles I strongly do NOT recommend

- Drug dealing. Jails, Institutions, and Death. That's where that will lead you. Just don't!
- Gambling. My great-grandfather was a professional riverboat gambler in the late 1800s. He went up and down the Mississippi River, earning money off the misfortune of others. He was extremely intuitive. He played against newer players who still hadn't discovered the real art of poker playing. But he also played against people more shrewd than him. When he lost all his money in a series of bad games, he committed suicide. I know it's a generalization fallacy to say that all poker players will end up this way, but it's a real danger. There are a lot of suicides in Las Vegas.
- Day Trading. Day Trading is a form of gambling, using the stock market like a

roulette wheel. The first time I heard of it was in a grim news story. A day trader had been purposely given a bad tip by his fellow traders, and he came to the trading office, shot everyone there, and killed himself. If you're reading this book, there's a strong chance you should avoid day trading.

Summing Up Side Hustles:

The key to a side hustle is figuring out what you love and doing it. Once you're doing it, figure out how you can make money at it instead of merely spending it. Never spend more on your hustle than you make doing it, or else it's a drain. Now get out there and hustle!

VOLUNTEERING

Do you have free time on your hands but can't afford to spend time pursuing your passions? Maybe your job drains you and keeps you so busy that you don't have an ounce of energy to spare. Either way, a surprising outlet exists that can put you in touch with the right network to start your side hustle or even lead to your dream job: volunteering.

While I was still in college studying Italian, our professor mentioned a volunteer opportunity. She said that a Sicilian puppet maker was coming to town and needed a translator for a talk he was giving. For some reason, the idea of puppets struck a note. As a kindergartner, I used to put on puppet shows for the family with my best friend. They were probably awful, but I still had a warm place in my heart for the art of puppetry. So I sheepishly raised my hand. It led to a job in the Italian Foreign Service!

How did that happen? Well, at the risk of boring you, I'll explain. The puppet show was presented by the

Italian Cultural Institute, a branch of the local consulate. I did a so-so job of translating, but it was good enough. Then the director of the Cultural Institute discovered that he wasn't allowed to employ volunteers. In a panic, he called me over to the office to write me a check for my services.

While I was there, I saw a clerk struggling with a clunky database called Q&A. It was ancient, but I had learned how to use it when I was a dispatcher for a phone sex service. I may have buried the lede there, but yes, I worked at a phone sex office during college. Anyway, I saw this poor clerk struggling, and I asked if I could help. I solved her problem.

When I turned around, the Director was staring at me, slack-jawed. In Italian he asked, "How do you know how to use that ancient piece of crap?"

I said, "I use it at my current job." Notice how I skillfully avoided mentioning that it was a job in the sex industry! I'm writing an entire book about financial discrimination in that industry, so don't think I'm judging. It's something I've experienced.

He asked, "Will you come work for me?" I did. And I enjoyed several years of hosting cultural events, art exhibits, food and film festivals, and, of course, working with that crusty old database to put their library and other archives in order.

The moral of this story is that sometimes, by giving something away, you will find that it comes back to you in unexpected ways. Not every volunteer job leads to employment, nor should it, but it does expose you to people working in a field that interests you. That often expands your network and makes you rich in social connections, which is how most jobs come about anyway!

GIGS

Gigs are financial band aids. They won't address your need for fulfillment, and they rarely lead to a satisfying career. The classic gig is driving for a ride-share or food delivery company. Yes, it will put money in your pocket quickly. No, it won't make you happy. Unless driving drunk people around town is your passion. If it's an emergency, get a gig on the side. The warning is that doing so will drain even more of your time, making it harder to start something that will really fulfill you. So don't do it forever. Maybe do it just long enough to pay off one credit card. And find a way to pursue your passions instead!

CHAPTER 7
WINDFALLS AND INHERITANCES

HELP! I'M RICH!

My financial advisor recently told me that because people born between 1945 and 1970 are the holders of the most wealth, there is about to be the biggest generational transfer of wealth in history between now and 2045. Nearly 85 trillion dollars is passing hands from grandparents, parents, uncles, aunts, and older friends to younger generations. It may be a small sum, or it might be a fortune, but many of you will someday receive money unexpectedly. It happened to me on a small scale when my grandmother, a schoolteacher, passed away. None of us knew she was sitting on money. Most of it went to her kids, but some of it went to her grandkids. This could happen to you, too. And it might not be a modest sum.

This is a windfall. A sum of money that blows in like the wind, unexpectedly, and falls into your lap. They come in many shapes, sizes, and flavors. They're not as rare as you may think. Whether it's finding a twenty-dollar bill on the sidewalk or winning the lottery, they're always a great way to get ahead, as I'll explain.

When a windfall happens, or if you win the lottery, you're going to need to know what to do. That's what this chapter is all about.

Here are some steps you should take right away:

Get a trustworthy Financial Advisor

Nobody knows what to do with your money better than somebody whose job it is to manage it. They will take your money and put it to work for you, making you immediately fall into the category of the wealthy. Because, as you remember, the definition of wealth is when your money makes you money without you doing a thing. As I've mentioned, I'll discuss advisors in more detail in Chapter 10.

Pay off your credit cards

Zero out all of your credit cards, and keep them in your freezer until you are ready to pay them off in full each month.

Buy a House

Remember that money my grandmother left me? It was just enough to put a 10% down payment on a house. My financial advisor said there was no better investment in my future than a low-interest mortgage. Rates were historically low, so I got a fixed mortgage. And I live there today.

I love my house. It felt very expensive at the time. We cut back on restaurants, travel, and other household expenses. Today, the mortgage is about one-third the going rate for a rental in Southern California. My husband and I earn more now, and we can afford some luxuries. The same could happen to you, especially if interest rates drop.

Don't tell your friends or extended family

You may have a solid group of trustworthy friends, but when word gets out you have money, you might find a few of them asking for handouts. It's incredibly awkward. Just remember that your financial situation is private. And your money is yours, so if word gets out and someone shows up asking for charity, the answer is "No." Sorry, I sound like a hard-ass, but that's the truth. It's none of their damn business, and your money is yours.

Here's something, though. Maybe you have a friend who is going through hard times. Maybe you have some stuff you need to get done but just don't have time or energy. You might want to pay them to help you. But don't go nuts. Help them out with meaningful work. See my segment below on having some to spend as you please.

A SAD ULTIMATUM

This is a truly sad tale, but it has value. I had a friend who worked hard and got promoted so high up at a tech company that she became a multi-millionaire and retired in her 40s. Friends noticed. One friend came around frequently asking her for money. She made the mistake of giving him some, and he came back again several times. Then my friend did something smart. She said, "I can give you what you're asking for, but if I do, we're no longer friends. If I don't, then we can remain friends as long as you never ask again." Sadly, he chose to take her money, and they never spoke again. But he had shown his true colors. A real friend knows better than to put you repeatedly in a painfully awkward position.

MONEY MIRACLE

SEE A PENNY, PICK IT UP

This is a woo-woo type of miracle, not the typical financial advice you'll get from a left-brained thinker. It's based on the law of attraction, which states that our mental state determines how our lives manifest. If we're feeling scarcity, we're living in a state of scarcity. If we feel abundance, we live in abundance.

I practice this in a small way. When I walk my dog, I come across pennies, nickels, dimes, quarters, and dollars. It doesn't matter if it's a penny or a twenty, I pick it up and thank the universe. We have a goblet full of coins near the front door. When my walk is over, the coin goes into the goblet. If it's paper money, it goes into a ceramic container that I found at the junk store. The container reads "Dreams".

By acknowledging any unexpected amount of money, we begin to pry open the door to prosperity. Don't leave a penny on the ground, and don't worry if it's face up or face down. It's wealth! It's money you didn't have to work for. Gratitude and the foresight to save any small windfall, as little as a penny, attracts more money.

———————————

Pay Yourself By Investing

Your financial advisor will help you invest your money. That money, as stocks and bonds, will start paying dividends and growing in value. You can cash out a large lump sum in an emergency, but you can probably just get by with the money trickling out and helping with bills, or maybe even paying enough to let you stop working for a while. This is what I mean by paying yourself.

DBIA (Don't Blow It All)

If you haven't seen it, I recommend watching the movie *To Leslie*. It's a true cautionary tale about a lottery winner who blows all of her winnings by drinking and drugging, giving it away, and ultimately winding up penniless. And I haven't really given away the plot - that's just the setting!

Watching it, you will see what happens if you don't have a plan for your money when it lands in your lap. There are hundreds of stories like Leslie's.

You may be thinking you should buy five brand new cars, a huge mansion in each of your favorite cities, or 500 pairs of Air Jordans. Or all of the above. Unless it's a ridiculously large sum in the tens of millions or greater, those are terrible ideas. I'll explain why.

You Can Have Some to Spend as You Please

I said "some". By "some," I mean you can spend maybe 5% of what you get on needless luxury items. Buying a mansion makes sense if you can do it with 5% of your inheritance. Buying more than one mansion is throwing away money.

On the other hand, you should buy a house if you don't already have one. I bought a modest house with 100% of my money, and it's worth three times what I paid for it. Mansions don't tend to appreciate much, because they're already overpriced.

Remember your spending plan? A windfall means you can buy yourself something nice. If you have nothing, living paycheck to paycheck, and suddenly you have something, then yes, it's okay to spend a little. However, buying stocks or rental properties makes more sense than buying luxury goods, whose value declines over time. And most of what you buy should be things that increase in value and/or pay dividends. But yes, you're entitled to splurge a little. Life is meant to be lived. A trip around the world, if you can afford it, is priceless. Giving to your favorite charity will enrich your life in ways that can't be priced. So figure out a budget and stick to it! Your financial advisor can help with this.

TAKEAWAYS

Windfalls can be blessings or curses depending on how you choose to spend them. Don't spend everything, and don't give it all away. Invest wisely with the help of an advisor. Give to causes that mean something to you, but don't give it all! Stick to 5% for splurging, and then sit back and reap the rewards of passive income from your investments.

CHAPTER 8
LUCK VS. PERSEVERANCE

WAITING FOR A WINDFALL

C hapter 7 suggested that you MAY have some money coming in. You never know, and you should NOT count on it while you're building wealth. It's not a plannable source of income unless you do something evil out of the plot of a Film Noir or True Crime drama. Don't be dastardly. You love your grandfather, and he should not die by ingesting an arsenic-laced birthday cake you prepared for him. You won't get a penny because you'll wind up in the slammer. Watch *Forensic Files* if you don't believe me.

Some of you are lucky enough to be getting financial assistance from your caregivers. And yet, you're reading this book. Why? Because you have to plan. You must persevere. Carry on until something changes for the better. A bonus at work might help, but not if you've already spent it when it arrives. The message is clear. Don't wait for a bonus.

MONEY MIRACLE

PLANNED BONUS

A client of mine was used to getting a bonus every quarter for her sales. She would carefully calculate her sales figures throughout the quarter and spend her check on credit cards before it arrived. Sometimes she spent it before realizing she wasn't going to get nearly the bonus she had planned for. A deal fell through, or a stubborn client waited to sign until after the quarter was over. It's no surprise that she came to me in debt and struggling to make ends meet, paycheck to paycheck.

After a few sessions, I was able to persuade her to budget everything without the bonus. When it came, she agreed to put half of the bonus into a brokerage account with her trusted financial advisor. With the other half, she would put 40% against her credit cards and take the remaining 10% as a reward for her hard work, spending it as she pleased. After a few quarters, she was surprised to see her brokerage account had grown, and her credit card payments were manageable. Instead of all her money going out, there was dividend money coming in! I explained dividends in Chapter 1, but as a reminder, they're money that companies give to their stockholders from their earnings. Her stocks paid dividends, which began to accumulate, and she reinvested them in a blended fund. She had wealth!

————————————————

Gambling

I mentioned this already, but gambling is a really bad way to aim for a windfall. Playing the Lotto has ridiculous odds. Yes, someone will win big. Some will win a few thousand. But 99.9999% of people playing will get absolutely nothing for their "investment".

Going to Vegas to parlay a thousand dollars into untold millions is a doomed plan. Windfalls from gambling can happen, and if they do, because you didn't take my advice, well, hats off to you. Please reread Chapter 7 so you don't blow it all!

Gambling takes many forms. Lotteries, casinos, but also risky ventures. If a bricklayer tells you that he has a surefire plan to make a fortune investing in gold, you should ask him if he lays gold bricks. If he doesn't know the first thing about gold, why would you take his advice? That's a surefire way to lose everything. I'll revisit this concept in Chapter 10.

Real investments pay off over time. Some become windfalls. Look at cryptocurrency. And don't worry if you don't understand it, because I don't really either. Just suffice it to say that everyone who bought into Bitcoin in 2016 was extremely rich by 2018. It was a good time to diversify that windfall by investing a significant portion of it in the stock market. It's true, if they hadn't, and held on until 2025, they would have five times more money today. But is that true of investors in FTX, a cryptocurrency that bit the dust in a huge way? More than half of all cryptocurrencies have failed, leaving their optimistic investors broke.

How many Bitcoin millionaires cashed out completely in 2019 (when the price dropped sharply for a while) and blew it on yachts, mansions, or sneakers? I don't have the figures, but I bet you couldn't throw a rock in San Francisco without hitting one of those former millionaires. And if it didn't, it would hit an unlucky person who invested their entire savings in a surefire penny stock that collapsed, eating their savings.

So invest wisely. Find an advisor, not a bricklayer. More about advisors in the last chapter.

Gambling is taking a risky action to attain a desired result. The lower the risk, the SLOWER your rewards. Fast money comes easily, and all too often goes out just as fast. Don't bet on your future, invest wisely. I can't say it enough times.

Black Swans

A black swan is an event so terrible and unexpected, it changes the landscape. Sometimes, everyone loses. At the time of this writing, tariffs have just caused EVERY INVESTOR, whether a billionaire or a clerk, to see the decline of one-third or more of the value of their stocks. But they lost it on paper. The losses aren't real unless they cash out the stock during the panic. Otherwise, they're still holding valuable investments that will eventually regain their value. I know this because I'm rather old. This isn't my first crash as an investor. Over time investors will see their money come back. In fact, there was a bounce back a few days later when some of the tariffs were reduced or put on hold. So hold on. When the market drops, that's actually a good time to buy.

In 1929, the Black Swan event was so intense that it caused everyone to lose faith in the value of their stocks. Everyone lost as one after another, companies went bankrupt. It happened once in the history of markets. Yes, it can happen again. But it is not as risky as putting all your savings on the roulette wheel in Vegas. Since 1932, a one-dollar investment in the top 500 stocks has grown to approximately $1,350.00. It's an average annual growth rate of 7% per year, compounded annually. But if you pulled out that money during dips and put it back in when the dip appeared to be over, you'd only have about $50.00. So when things get bad, HOLD. Don't panic and sell. The odds that the market will crash out of existence is microscopic. The odds that your roulette investment in Vegas will crash out of existence is about 99.99%.

My Ship Will Come In

I read tarot cards. It was just something my wacky mother taught me as a kid, but they have a lot of power when you understand them. This segment is about the Three of Wands. In the Rider-Waite deck (the most popular), the Three of Wands depicts a man standing on a hillside, watching ships in the harbor. There are many interpretations. Some people say the ships are his, and he's watching his massive fortune arrive in the harbor. Others talk about how the ships are not his; he's still waiting for his to arrive, wasting a lot of time watching the horizon instead of preparing for when they finally return from overseas and tie up at the docks. This is about that latter interpretation.

If you're invested in well-diversified funds, your ship is a slow boat from the far East. It's moving at a snail's pace, and you have plenty of time to wait for your fortune. You will have it, as sure as that man's ships will arrive, but you have so much else to do while you're waiting. Side hustles, salary increases - these are the way you will get out of debt in the present moment.

MONEY MIRACLE

CONTRARY ACTION

In 1999, Apple stock was faltering. My grandmother, a grade school teacher, had invested a portion of her savings in Apple Stock. She'd been advised to do so by my cousin, who worked in the tech industry and knew it was a good, solid investment. He'd met Steve Jobs personally and believed in his vision. Apple was under water (worth less than she'd paid) that year. She decided to sell it. Before she did, though, she called her grandson (my cousin) to let him know. He told her something wise. "Don't sell, buy more." That is what is called contrary action. She didn't listen and sold most of it. Obviously, when the iPod and later the iPhone were introduced, Apple stock flourished. She cashed out the shares she'd held on to and bought diversified funds. That was a safe course of action, and her money grew over time. If she'd held on or even bought more like my cousin advised, she'd have been a multimillionaire. She didn't. This is an example of taking gold investment advice from someone who deals in gold, not a bricklayer. It's still a bit of a gamble, but the rewards are more likely. She certainly didn't die penniless, but she could have had more than she did.

HARD WORK VERSUS SMART WORK

This chapter is about perseverance. It means you can't count on luck. You can count on perseverance. Taking the measures I outlined in the early chapters is a painful and slow process. However, it's the most reliable and likely way to get out of debt and into wealth.

To that end, I would like to discuss the 80/20 rule. It states that 80% of your results come from 20% of your efforts. This principle is used frequently by Chief Operations Officers in large companies. They identify where they're working too hard and refocus their efforts on those that bring in greater returns.

How does this apply to personal finances? I'm going to give a controversial answer - it doesn't really apply.

If you're struggling with your personal finances, it may be because you're only focusing on the 20% that yields 80%. This means you stay at your current job because it's easy. It means you don't take extra steps to generate additional income. You settle for 80% of the results at a time when you can't afford to!

A side hustle is an example of working harder to get beyond 80%. Yes, you're going to scurry about to scrape together a few hundred extra. Is that wasted effort? No.

Dead End?

If your full-time job is with a company you dislike, or involves something you don't want to do, then you should probably give them 20% of your energy for 80% of the results. The 80/20 rule applies to dead-end jobs. When you pick the right tasks, you'll be more productive than most of your coworkers! You'll have a better work-life balance. Don't spend a second doing more than enough at a thankless but necessary job. Do enough.

Give more effort to your side hustle. Your side hustle should feed your soul. It should be something to which, if you lost your current job, you would gladly devote all your time and energy. It's the hustle that will make your dreams come true if it pays off.

Great Job? Good Growth Potential?

HOWEVER, if you've decided your current corporate job has a career path that leads to well-paid, fulfilling work, then you should give as close to 100% as you can at work. But be sure that the extra 80% of effort is devoted to doing things your bosses will notice. Don't spend extra time on thankless work. Figure out what gets your extra effort in front of the people who can help your career.

Maybe you've already been promoted once where you are. I have bad news - most people only get one promotion. If you've identified a corporate job at a different company for which you're qualified, devote some spare energy to the hustle to get hired there. Maybe it's a job that pays the same, but it's in a different part of the company that interests you more. Maybe it's a higher-paying job in an area you currently work in. However, take this time-honored advice when you do apply, so that your job search effort pays off. The advice is as follows: don't apply for a higher-level job in an area that you don't currently work in. Be prepared to leave your current company.

Either apply for a higher-level job at another corporation in the position and industry in which you currently excel, or try to move into an area at your current company that aligns better with your interests, then apply for a similar or higher-level job at a corporation that interests you more.

Don't try to do both! In other words, don't try to switch industries at a higher level. If you do, you'll always be struggling to win out against someone with more experience and higher qualifications. It's one or the other. Switch industries at your current level, or apply in your current area of expertise at a different company. Once you are ensconced in the new job, it's much easier to either move up or move across.

This is a tricky scenario to describe, so I've done my best to illustrate it for you.

You don't like your job, company, or how much you make?

It is easier to get a low level job in a new department or company. This will allow to feel happier at work

Once you are in a position you like, ask for a promotion, but keep in mind you will likely only be promoted once at the company where you are now.

If you have already been promoted, you need to apply for a higher level job in your current department, at a different company

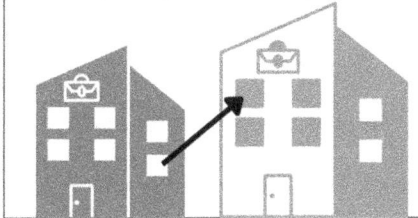

If you took a similar level job at a new company in the area that interests you, focus on impressing your bosses and getting promoted. If you took a higher-level job in the department you already know, it's time to take some classes to prove you can move across at your higher level to your area of interest.

Switching industries requires identifying your "transferable" skills. If you're in accounting in a boring industry, find an accounting job in an exciting industry. You can always apply internally to get out of your boring position into one that is far more interesting.

If you're in accounting and enjoy your current industry, and you were already promoted once, consider applying for a higher-level accounting position within the same industry. That's how you get that "second" promotion, and eventually a third. Don't stay loyal to a company that doesn't appreciate you!

If you love what you do, you'll have to give 100% until you reach your desired position. Once you love your job, and it pays what you need, then you can kick back and do less. That's why hard work is needed before you can apply the 80/20 rule to your work life. The key is perseverance.

TAKEAWAYS

Gambling is taking a risk for an unlikely outcome. A five-dollar lottery ticket is a small but poorly spent risk. Putting your entire savings into a "sure thing" single stock or currency is a huge risk with very poor odds as well. If your friend is involved in the industry and knows the value of the company, it's less of a risk, but you should never devote your entire savings to a single stock.

Perseverance is the opposite of gambling. You give your time and energy to things that may not reward you immediately, but will surely reward you over time. Persevering at work is a good idea if you love your company and the industry. Persevering is also a good idea if you want to switch jobs and/or industries, because your odds of being able to move to another company or another industry are increased if you do well in your current job. Be mindful of how much energy you are devoting to work. The 80/20 rule applies immediately if you're in a job that will never get you closer to your dreams. Give the rest of the energy to your side hustle. 80/20 also applies once you've found your dream job and are happy there. You should devote as much of your energy to achieving your dreams, whether that comes through a side hustle or moving up the ladder in your chosen field.

CHAPTER 9
AUTOMATE YOUR LIFE

This is probably my favorite chapter. There is nothing better than turning your financial affairs over to autopilot. If you've been used to living with a scarcity mindset, this might frighten you. However, once you have a clear picture of how much you have and when more is expected to arrive, you can start to automate everything. You've been consulting your money tracking app regularly, so you know what you spend each month. This will be easy once you're solvent and earning a sufficient income. If you're still struggling to earn more than you spend, this chapter doesn't apply yet!

Automatic Bill Pay With a Dash of Gratitude

Here's something you might think is insane. I'm grateful for my bills. I learned this years and years ago, when I was in my early 20s. You may groan when each bill comes in, but in truth, you should feel grateful. You must realize, it's an incredibly fortunate situation when a company trusts you to pay them later. The power company has extended you the opportunity to receive their services, and they trust you to pay them. How nice is that?

What I love is that not only do they trust you, but

they give you an opportunity to trust them. You can go to your power company's website and sign up to have them automatically debit your checking account each month via your debit card. How dangerous is that, though? If you have no prudent reserve in your checking account, it's pretty risky. Those bills can be staggering, depending on the time of year and which climate you live in.

Automatic payments work best for items whose amount doesn't change very often. Let's examine what you can and cannot automate.

Automate these bills but keep an eye on them for increases or decreases:

- Subscriptions (review often)
  - Streaming
  - Memberships
  - Music
  - Apps and Software
  - Meal Kit Delivery
- Phone
- Internet
- Gym membership
- Insurance
  - Health
  - Car
- Level Pay Utilities

If you're still paying down your credit cards:

- Credit Card Payments that are above the minimum, as explained in chapter 3.

- Minimum payments on everything else

DON'T AUTOMATE:

- Utility bills that aren't level pay because your utility doesn't offer it.
- Subscriptions you plan to cancel after a month or two

Here's the rub - most of you are following my advice to use only debit cards. Automating your payments should start small, just a few things, and you need to put it in your calendar so you know when it's happening.

Some day in the future, maybe a few months, maybe a few years, you'll be ready to switch to credit cards, because you will have developed the habit of paying your credit cards in full, as I explained in Chapter 3. Credit cards can absorb the shock of a big bill, provided they are paid in full each billing cycle.

MONEY MIRACLE

LEVEL PAY

In Los Angeles, our electric usage is negligible in the winter when we heat our house with gas, and staggering in the summer when our air conditioner runs non-stop. Or at least that was how it was until they finally started trusting their customers enough to do a level payment plan. The Los Angeles Department of Water and Power (LADWP) was the worst bill we had. They only billed every two months. So when those summer bills came in, they sometimes topped $1,000.00! We had to watch our finances carefully during the summer, and we never signed up for autopay to avoid a budget error that could lead to overdrafts.

Finally, LADWP listened to its customers, many of whom were defaulting on their bills because of the draconian, outdated billing practices. We signed up for a level payment with automatic debit from our checking account. The amount is rather high, but it remains consistent, and it occurs once a month. We pay more than we used to in the winter, but much less in the summer. At last, we could ignore the bills and know that our automatic payments would come out like clockwork, always at the same time, for the same amount. Once a year, they rebalance. That is the only time we need to pay close attention to the bill, and the increase is never more than fifty dollars. And once every so often, it actually goes down a little!

———————————

Automated Loan Pay

Loans differ slightly from bills. They're almost always the same amount each month. You can stop paying some of them, but most are unavoidable. They can all be automated, but if the dollar amounts are really high, you may need to pay them manually based on the timing of your paychecks. If you're doing well, then an automated loan payment can take your mind off that bill.

You can automate all of these if you have the habit of checking your balances:

- Rent or Mortgage
  - If you own a house, use an escrow account to bundle taxes, insurance, and mortgage
  - Some services exist that let you pay your rent with credit/debit cards
- Car payments
- Student Loans

A QUICK WORD ABOUT STUDENT LOANS

Student loans are the worst. Banks made a deal with the government that allows them to lend to people who, at the time of the loan, could never possibly repay them. The traditional rationale is that after college, the student will start earning enough to pay them back. These loans may be the reason you're suffering. Credit cards can be ignored, but student debt never, ever goes away on its own. You must pay, or you will be forever in a growing pile of debt.

Education is extremely valuable. Student loans are the primary means by which most people in the US can afford an education. I took out loans for my undergraduate education, and it took me a long time to pay them off.

I wish I had a really solid piece of advice for you here, but this is what I can say. A good education is priceless. Debt is the shittiest outcome of a good education. Can you get a scholarship and grants? Can you do work-study? Can you attend an affordable community college for a couple of years before transferring to a state university? Can you get into one of the Ivy League colleges that have stopped charging tuition? Ask yourself these things before figuring out how much of a loan you will need to get through college.

Automate Your Savings - Hide Money From Yourself

I mentioned this concept in Chapter 2. If you're going to keep 10% of all you earn, you need a solid way to live up to that promise. Enter automated savings.

On your bank's website, you will see an automated recurring transfers feature. If you've followed my earlier advice, you will have already set up a savings account. If you haven't, now is the time to do it. After about five mouse clicks and identifying some motorcycles and traffic lights, you'll have a savings account!

Next, navigate to the Automated Transfers section. They will walk you through the simple process of setting up a sweep from checking to savings.

To ease into it, start with a very small amount at first. It might be $10.00 or $25.00. It really depends on your paycheck. You're going to make sure the sweep happens the day after your paycheck arrives. That way, you will never incur an overdraft fee. Some banks are considerate and have a clause that prevents them from performing the sweep if it would cause your balance to drop below $0.00. Other banks are ruthless mercenaries, surviving entirely on the financial misery of others. If the Terms and Conditions are in a microscopic font, you may need to contact a chatbot and escalate to a human to determine the penalty for attempting an automated sweep with insufficient funds. But find out. It might be time to switch banks.

The small amount you sweep is not the final figure, but it's enough for the present. You need to see it proven out that by "hiding" this money from yourself, you won't even feel it. It's painless to set aside a few dollars every paycheck. As you grow more comfortable, you'll increase it. And remember, it's yours to KEEP, not yours to spend. It will function like an emergency fund, but you need to identify a true emergency.

Examples of real emergencies:

- No groceries with imminent starvation
- Job loss
- Bail bonds for you or your immediate family
- A non-working car that you need to get to work
- A leak or other detrimental home repair crisis
- A trip to a distant family funeral

Examples of non-emergencies:

- Dining out with friends
- Vacation
- Bail for a friend or non-nuclear family member
- Any car repairs when you can take public transportation
- Shelf paper for your closet
- Flowers for funerals
- Birthday anything
- Family reunions (this may be a relief)

You need to be clear whether something is an emergency. You need to be direct with the friend who claims that their unfortunate-but-not-deadly situation is life-threatening. You need to patiently explain that you're taking concrete steps to repair your finances, and you cannot afford it. Don't pretend you can. Be honest. A good friend or family member will understand.

Automate Your Investing

Remember that extremely boring segment in chapter three about 401(k) plans? Now is a good time to reread it. If you still don't understand what a 401(k) plan is, you're not alone. I didn't know until I asked around. It sounded dumb. "Why on earth would I take money out of my paycheck and put it in the stock market? I need that money now, not when I'm 65!" That was My initial thought. But there's a similar principle at play as in the automatic savings. You hide money from yourself, and it turns out not to be that much. You don't pay any payroll taxes on it now, which means that even though you've taken, say, $100.00 out of your paycheck, it will only feel like $70.00 because of the tax savings.

Years later, when you are old enough to withdraw it, you will pay income tax on the money you put in - but you don't pay ANY taxes on the amount the money grew while it was in the account (also known as capital gains taxes). So you end up making some tax-free money in the stock market, which is great.

MONEY MIRACLE

AUTOMATED INVESTING

When I signed on with my first financial advisor, he asked me to put aside a monthly amount to grow my brokerage account (non-retirement money). We landed on a sum that seemed outrageous to me at the time. It was almost 7% of my take-home pay! What!?!? How would I ever afford that? My paychecks were tight after all the taxes and medical insurance. That was a big chunk of my income.

But I relented. The money served two purposes. First, I had to pay my advisor an annual fee for managing my money. That might sound like a rip-off, but it's well worth it. The second purpose was to build up an emergency fund. See, I only owed him about half of what he was taking. The remaining funds were deposited into a money market account. A money market account is simply a flashy name for a savings account with slightly higher interest rates. The money he left in there earned a small bit of interest. And eventually, I just forgot about it. Flash forward six years. My car was struck and totaled, and the insurance company only offered its replacement value, which wasn't enough for a good used car, let alone a new one. I didn't want big car payments. I vaguely remembered that I had an emergency fund with my advisor, so I called him. Lo and behold, I had socked away more than enough to cover the difference between the insurance payout and the price of a good used car. I still drive it today.

———————————

Automate Your Account Inquiries With Apps

I mentioned this already and told you to go out and get a money-tracking app, such as NerdWallet, Quicken Simplifi or YNAB, and learn how to use it. If you properly connect all your accounts, you will instantly know where your money is and how much you have. In the old days, you also had to figure out how many checks were floating out there that hadn't been cashed. These days, it's extremely rare to pay anything by check. So it's WYSIWYG - what you see is what you get. You're looking at a live snapshot of all your money and where it sits, where it's going, what you're doing with it. Some of the accounts only update once a day, so it's a snapshot of the previous day. But still, it's amazing!

Imagine how difficult that was, even just 25 years ago! Online banking started in the late 1990s. It helped a lot, but it wasn't until the mid-2000s that software became available to track one's financial life. Many banks and payment systems that we take for granted today were unavailable, particularly with cash apps and small, regional banks. You just couldn't get a good picture. I had to use check registers, spreadsheets, and good old-fashioned pen and paper to figure out what I was spending and where. So it behooves you to learn how to use one of the apps and check it frequently to see if your wealth is increasing or decreasing. It will show you exactly where you spend that money, for the most part. Sometimes it guesses wrong, and you have to fix it. The app will help you find fraud. I had a client who was paying nearly $500.00 a month in fraudulent PayPal charges and didn't know because he didn't have the app! We found it and fixed it immediately.

MONEY MIRACLE

THE OBSERVER EFFECT

Your money tracking app will give you a clear picture of where you're spending money, and where you're getting it. It will tell you how deep in debt you are, or how much your positive net worth has grown. There is a phenomenon in Quantum Physics called "The Observer Effect." It turns out that by simply observing a particle, you can change its behavior.

Money tracking apps do the same thing! Remember that most money (other than cash and coins) is not something you physically touch - it's an idea, represented by figures on a balance sheet. When you observe how your money is being spent, you influence how you behave with it. You will see that you spent $450.00 on ride shares when you could have taken the bus, and you will think, "I guess I should try taking the bus more often." When you see that you spent $50.00 on groceries and $1,000.00 on meals, you'll think, "Holy crap, I need to cook more often!" And lo and behold, you begin to do that. You "find" money because you stop spending as much. That's the Observer Effect.

Get Better at Tracking

I can't possibly teach you in this ebook how to become a power user of money-tracking apps like Nerd-Wallet, Simplifi or YNAB. Luckily, we live in an age where there are pages and pages of instructions, videos, and forums that allow you to learn in your preferred learning mode how to become an expert. You'll even learn how to start tracking paper money, which isn't always easy with an app. You'll learn how to set a budget and adjust it as you find how inaccurate it is. You'll get accurate, real-time warnings about when you're about to scrape bottom. You might even get little badges for paying down your credit cards.

The trick to making these cash apps into true magic is to learn how to use them like an expert, and then use them daily. I open mine every morning while I have a cup of tea. I look to see how I'm doing. I play around with the budget if I'm bored. Some of the apps even gamify the experience, inspiring you to do better and win the challenge of managing personal finances. Imagine a game where winning means you acquire true wealth. That's the best prize there is.

CHAPTER 10
PUTTING IT ALL TOGETHER

...WHEN YOUR MONEY PAYS YOU MONEY

I n this book, I taught you the meaning of wealth. We learned that true Wealth with a capital W is not what you make at your job, nor what luxury items you possess. It's simply when your money pays you money. If you've reached this chapter and still don't understand what I mean by 'money paying you money,' I've failed. You cannot measure your wealth by active income, which is the money you make toiling away for the man, or at your small business. That income can become wealth if you manage it right, but it IS NOT WEALTH. Period. It's just cash flow. The Prada bag, the Maserati, or the Rolex are status symbols, but they aren't wealth. Someone who wants to signal a belief that they are wealthy might spend lavishly and show off. But that doesn't mean they have real wealth.

Once I defined wealth for you in Chapter One, I moved on to the current financial emergency. I started triage. We need to stop the bleeding. Not a single person I've worked with wasn't in need of immediate first aid when they came to me. So don't feel bad if you realize you're upside down. It just means you're part of the 99%.

Triage means we patch up the most severe wounds

first and then address the minor cuts and bruises later. Credit cards are usually the worst culprit. First, you stick them into the freezer in a tub of water! Next, you look at the details to find every place your cards are leaking money: subscriptions, ride shares, anywhere you just spend and don't think about it. You patch those leaks with a debit card. It sucks. You feel poor. You likely realize you STILL have serious financial wounds that need to heal. You overspend, underearn, and rack up debt. But just freezing your credit cards in a tub of water is huge!

It's hard to see where it's all going without that expense tracking app, so you should download it and set it up right away. You may not know how to use all its features, but you can teach yourself later. For now, you just need a snapshot of where all your money went and how much you owe. You need a single place to see what's going right and what's going wrong. That's triage. You can come back and become an expert once you've finished fixing the bleeding everywhere else.

Now that you can identify the sources of the problems and have a diagnosis, you can begin treating them. You make yourself coffee. You buy groceries. You cancel all but one of your gym memberships. You do the same with your streaming services. This may be enough. If it isn't, you get more tools later in the book, like side hustles, to help bridge the gap.

The next step in Chapter Three is to actively pay down your credit cards, now that you're not using them. As you may recall, you pay the LOWEST balance first. Why? Because it's an upside-down strategy that comes with a rapid sense of accomplishment. It may cost you more in the short term, but it speeds up the process of getting out of debt. You get to celebrate much sooner, which is incredibly inspiring.

When your credit begins to heal, you'll get a lot of 0% interest offers. These are actually not half bad. They usually charge you 3% interest to make the transfer, but it's not as much as the interest on a 29.99% APY balance, so the transfer makes sense. You just have to be sure to pay it down before the interest jumps back up after 6-18 months.

Until those credit cards are paid off, you're going to have a hard time building wealth. You spent a few years getting into this hole, so you may need a few to climb back out. But you can do it!

Student loans are the darkest, scariest credit problem out there. You need to do everything you can to pay them off.

The comedian David Sedaris has a routine about Sallie Mae, the credit agency responsible for servicing student loans. He said that she sounds like a sweet, naive country girl, the kind your folks want you to marry. But once you do, she turns on you and becomes a vicious, spiteful bully. If you've gotten hitched to Sallie Mae, there's no tricks you can pull. With credit cards, you can just stop paying them. They can't do much to you for a few years, after which they might take you to court at the very worst. Sallie Mae is sitting on a perch like a black widow spider, waiting to charge you huge penalties and interest every time you trip up. And it never goes away!

Even while you are paying down your credit, you need to do whatever you can to set aside savings. In Chapter 4, I talked about the ideal figure of 10% of every paycheck. If things are tight, you can split that between your 401(k) (~6%) and your savings account (~4%), or less if it makes the difference between starving and eating. You can ease into it gradually if it's too painful. Making the savings deposit automatic, particularly by splitting your direct deposit, you will find that it doesn't hurt much. You can increase it as you go. This is so that you can have a three-month emergency fund and, eventually, put money in the stock market, where dividends make you rich.

In Chapter 5, I introduced the concept of a spending

plan vs. a budget. You are choosing how to spend your money. A budget says, "You can't have this." A spending plan says, "You need this, and you can have a little of this." By sorting out your discretionary and non-discretionary expenses, it becomes easy to build a spending plan. Rent is non-negotiable; you must pay it. Period. A restaurant is nice, and if you can add it to your spending plan without upsetting the balance, then go for it. Maybe you'd rather spend it on a weekend getaway. Can you fit it into your spending plan? Perhaps if you cut down on eating out, you can. Eventually, you can even do it all. But maybe not today, unless you're a high earner with a lot of needless expenses you can trim. But no matter how much you earn, part of that money is to save, and part of it is to spend on things you want, not just those you need.

Chapter 6 discusses a condition known as Underearning. There are organizations that have identified Underearning as a disease, much like alcoholism and addiction. It's not the same as laziness or lack of ambition. Underearning is a symptom of low self-worth. You may scramble and work harder than anyone you know, but you don't know how to turn that into high earnings. You might be making pipe cleaners into Christmas ornaments. You deserve to earn more! You have value more than you can imagine. Don't scramble around for Abe Lincoln pennies when you could be making Benjamins.

Working doing something you love makes you rich in ways you can't imagine. A side hustle that indulges one of your passions and makes you extra cash is a form of wealth. You're working for it, but it's feeding your soul. A gig, on the other hand, is more of an emergency measure. Gigs should be temporary fixes until you can find a good side hustle that enriches your life.

Could your ship come in? Could you suddenly have a million dollars? Yes. Chapter 7 was about windfalls. They happen suddenly and often unexpectedly. You need to be ready to deal with it. Many of you have never had that kind of money, and don't know what to do to keep it and make more of it. That's where a Financial Advisor comes in. And yes, I will get more in-depth about financial advisors in a minute. Your advisor should be the first person you call when a windfall lands in your lap. They know better than anyone what you should be doing with it. Whether it's buying a house or paying off high-interest loans and credit cards, there are right things you can do, and wrong things. Avoid the wrong things; resist the urge to blow it all on crazy shit.

In Chapter 8, you learned about luck. You think no ship can come in if you don't gamble. You might be right, but it's the wrong approach. Your ship might take ten slow years to come in. If you try to send a ship to gather goods overnight (which is like placing a bet on the roulette wheel), it's more likely to sink than make it. Stop betting on your future! Invest wisely.

Turning your money life around from one of debt and underearning to a life of wealth and prosperity can begin immediately. The results may take a long time, but you can change the trajectory in a few quick steps. The hardest part is staying on track and waiting months or years for the turnaround to be completed. If you have the money tracking app, you'll be able to see it every day. Is your net worth positive or negative? When the day arrives that you reach a positive net worth, plan a celebration. Perhaps not a costly round-the-world cruise, but perhaps a nice dinner out that will not put you back into negative net worth!

Chapter 9 talks about the beauty of bills. You can feel gratitude that a company trusted you, but you don't have to spend as much time thinking about them as you currently do. Once you have righted your ship, you can put all your bills on debit cards (or, if you have the dis-cipline, credit cards) and stop thinking about them!

Your money-tracking app will alert you if you don't have enough funds for a recurring bill.

Chapter 9 also talks about the ease with which you can 'hide' the 10 percent savings I mentioned in Chapter 4. Sweeps, automatic transfers, 401(k) plans – they all make it easy for you to 'keep' your earnings before you spend them.

If you've read this far, you understand money better than 99% of the population. Even the very, very wealthy might not understand these concepts, and therefore risk losing their wealth. Now that you have this knowledge, put the miracles to work for you today. Visualize a future where you no longer have to work for someone else. Envision wealth: your money is the source of your income. You can do the work you were born to do. And unlike some folks who inherit or stumble into wealth, you'll know what to do to stay wealthy. You'll know how to automate your finances so you don't spend a ridiculous amount of time managing your money. You'll be free from debt, and prospering.

As your Guncle Duncan, I want you to enjoy financial freedom. I found my way from debt and despair to financial well-being, and you can, too. And remember, even if you're earning a lot of money, you can still be broke if you're spending more than you earn. Rein in your expenses, stick to your spending plan, pay attention to your money, stop gambling, and you will find your way to wealth and well-being.

AS PROMISED - ALL ABOUT FINANCIAL ADVISORS

You've heard me mention financial advisors throughout this book. What are they? Think of them as a money therapist. If they're good, they'll counsel you, reassure you, praise your efforts, and generally fix your broken relationship with money. If they're so-so, they'll at least offer you advice on what to do with your money. You can always switch "therapists" to a better advisor if the one you have isn't doing the trick.

I am not a certified financial advisor, so I can't ethically make recommendations on which stocks to pick, how much to put into the market, or any of the other things that an advisor will do for you.

How do you get one? Many of you have little or no savings, so you believe a financial advisor wants nothing to do with you. That's not true. A good advisor will offer to talk to you and give you further advice on how to start your savings. They'll tell you to come back when you've got a nest egg. And it can be a tiny nest egg. I'd say $5,000.00 in your savings account might be enough. If all you do is stop drinking expensive coffee every day and put that money in a savings account, you'll have that much in just a year or two!

For those of you who took my advice and started contributing to a 401(k) at work, you may already have a financial advisor through the firm that holds your retirement savings, without even realizing it. This is often a perk with 401(k) plans. These advisors may be very good, or they may not be the best, but they're free money therapists. Would you turn down free therapy if it helped you get a handle on your mental well-being? I doubt it. So don't turn down a free financial advisor.

I found my advisor when I lost my job. I had a tiny 401(k) that needed to be "rolled over" into an IRA (Individual Retirement Account). "Rolling over" is a term you'll hear in the HR office right before you are handed your box of stuff from your desk and escorted out of the building. I didn't know what it meant when they said it, so I'm going to assume you don't know either. If you do, skip the next paragraph.

You are only allowed to put money into a 401(k) when you are working as an employee at a company that has the plan. If you quit or get fired, your plan freezes. It still earns interest, but you can't make changes to it or add anything else. That is when you have to move it to another 401(k) at a new job, or, better yet, into an IRA. The Individual Retirement Account is independent from your workplace, so you can contribute to it when you're not contributing to a 401(k). You can try to do it on your own through an online brokerage, but it's way better to have it with a financial advisory firm. They'll do so much better than you could ever do on your own.

With my advisory, I grew that tiny, miserable 401(k) into a rather impressive IRA over time. Any time I quit or got let go (which was pretty often, frankly), I'd roll the present 401(k) into the IRA, and start a new 401(k) whenever I found another job. If the job didn't offer a 401(k) option, I'd put money into an IRA when I could. And the financial advisor helped me automate the process. He would pull a small portion of my earnings from my checking account at the beginning of each month and deposit it into a type of savings account I mentioned earlier called a money market account. The interest was pretty small, but it was better than a bank savings account. Automating the transfer made it easy to save up.

I hope you'll seek out a financial advisor now, regardless of your current financial situation. They will help you in this process of moving from a life of debt and survival to a thriving, successful existence. If you find an advisor who's willing to work with you at this very early stage, you've probably found a winner. If you see them in person, check their wall for awards and plaques. Maybe their firm is rated on a review site. Maybe you just get a really good vibe when you talk to them. If they're certified, they're bound by a code of ethics. But the best kind wouldn't need that code to do the right thing for you and your money.

AFTERWORD

Let's review the most important concepts in the book to cement them in your mind. I have probably repeated myself enough, but I'll risk it and say it all again in summary fashion.

Remember that becoming wealthy is a process, some of which takes years. Taking actions outlined in this book can and will make your life much better right away. And they're not difficult.

Take stock of your expenses. Get a money app and see what you're earning and where you're spending it. Fix it. Remember the accounting concept of discretionary and fixed (non-discretionary) expenses. You can't do much about fixed expenses like rent, but you can adjust discretionary expenses, like coffee.

Freeze your cards. Stop spending more than you earn. The only way to do that is with credit cards. Stick them in the freezer, literally. Decide if you want to take a credit vacation. If you are spending even one penny more than you are getting paid, you are going in the wrong direction.

Ten percent of all you earn is yours to keep. That's a quote right out of my favorite money book, "The Richest Man in Babylon." Remembering that "keep" is not the same as "spend", you'll recall that it means you should set aside ten percent of your earnings. Initially, that money is there for emergencies, such as job loss or prolonged illnesses. After it reaches a certain point, that money is for investing. And that is when wealth starts to kick in and grow.

When you take steps to earn more than you spend, you will have to give up some of your favorite things. But you must plan to spend some of your money on living well. You don't need two gyms, but you may need one. You don't need caviar, but you need groceries. That's a spending plan. You find the things you love, decide on a few that get to stay in your spending plan, and put the rest on hold.

Not everyone reading this book is an underearner. Some of you are making six figures and spending it just as quickly as you earn it. For you high earners, if you take some of the steps in here, your finances will improve immediately. It will be painless. This book is written for high earners and low earners alike. For the folks who are still struggling to gain experience and find a well-paying job, there are things you can do about it. Ask for a raise. Most bosses don't think about it until you put the thought in their heads. You can take on side hustles doing things you love, which might eventually become a career. You can take on gigs that help get you out of the hole, doing something easy like driving a car or babysitting. There are plenty of ways for low earners to get on the right track.

If a big pile of money lands in your lap, don't rush out and spend it. Invest it. Let the money earn money. It's a great time to find a financial advisor if you don't already have one. Do not become a tragic lottery winner. Be sensible. Hopefully, the principles you learned in this book will kick in, and you'll understand that it isn't the pile of cash that makes you rich. It's what you do with it. Let your money pay you!

Gambling is not a solid plan for getting wealthy. In fact, it's a plan to become poor! Whether it's literal Vegas-style gambling or betting on the stock market, you're extremely unlikely to "strike it rich". Especially if you're taking stock tips from guys at the beach. Waiting for a windfall can put your life on hold forever. Luck is wonderful, but fleeting. Skill is enduring. Don't bet on your future. Make wise decisions with the help of a trusted advisor. And stick to the plans you made in earlier chapters.

Automating your finances eliminates guesswork, saves tons of time, and gives you the freedom to pursue more interesting things. Financial tracking apps help you stay on top of things; automatic savings, bill pay, and investing keep the whole engine running. It may take time to get your financial boat fully upright and able to sail into automated payments. Automation requires a certain cash cushion to avoid ugly surprises. That's why I put it near the end of the book. It's the next step after you are solvent with some savings.

I hope the advice I've given will set you on the right course. I'm offering you the kind of guidance your parents might not have had the time or knowledge to impart. I didn't learn ANY of these principles from my parents or school. I had to read books like this one and figure out how to get right with my money. But I did. As someone who has been penniless and without a roof over his head, I can attest that these principles can help anyone get back on their feet and begin the long road to wealth and happiness.

—Guncle Duncan

ABOUT THE AUTHOR

CONNECT WITH ME!

Thank you for reading *Money Magic: Easy and Surprising Ways to Not Be Broke*! Did you find it helpful? I welcome all reader feedback and would love to hear your thoughts.

If *Money Magic* offered strategies that helped you think about money differently, I would greatly appreciate it if you would post a review for this book so it may reach more readers like you:

Post a review on Amazon or Goodreads
I would love to stay in touch with you. You can learn more about what I do at the following links:
My website: duncanwritesbooks.com
Jim Dandy Publishing: jimdandypublishing.com
Books That Save Lives: booksthatsavelives.net

instagram.com/duncanjimdandy
linkedin.com/in/dunkie
amazon.com/author/duncanmacleod
goodreads.com/duncanwritesbooks

Books That Save Lives came into being in 2024 when the editor and publisher, Brenda Knight, heard directly from readers and authors that certain self-help, grief, psychology books, and journals were providing a lifeline for folks. We live in a stressful world where it is increasingly difficult not to feel overwhelmed, worried, depressed, and downright scared. We intend to offer support for the vulnerable, including people struggling with mental wellness and physical illness as well as people of color, queer and trans adults and teens, immigrants and anyone who needs encouragement and inspiration.

From first responders, military veterans, and retirees to LGBTQ+ teens and to those experiencing the shock of bereavement and loss, our books have saved lives. To us, there is no higher calling.

We would love to hear from you! Our readers are our most important resource; we value your input, suggestions, and ideas.

Please stay in touch with us and follow us at:
www.booksthatsavelives.net
Instagram: @booksthatsavelives